THE
DIVINE MOTHER
SPEAKS

love +
celebration!

THE
DIVINE MOTHER
SPEAKS

The Healing of the
HUMAN HEART

RASHMI KHILNANI

Foreword by Leonard Orr

RAINBOW RIDGE
PUBLISHING

Cover and Interior design by Frame 25 Productions
Cover photograph © emferr c/o Shutterstock.com

If you are unable to order this book from your local
bookseller, you may order directly from the publisher.

Rainbow Ridge Publishing
140 Rainbow Ridge Road
Faber, Virginia 22938
434-361-1723

Visit the author at:
www.reiki-energy-mastery.com

Library of Congress Cataloging-in-Publication Data applied for.

ISBN 978-0-9844955-0-4

10 9 8 7 6 5 4 3 2 1

Printed on acid-free paper in the United States

DEDICATION

I DEDICATE THIS BOOK to my beloved late father, Mr. K. C. Khanna, former resident editor of the *Times of India*, who taught me to help all Beings who crossed my path without any expectation of return and that books make wonderful best friends!

And to my darling challenging "larger-than-life" mother, Amrit Khanna, who taught me always to be brave no matter what life throws at you and to keep the "hat of one's sense of humor firmly on one's head."

And most of all, this book is a prayer of love and gratitude to the immortal Christ Yogi Babaji and the Divine Mother in her many myriad forms.

December, 2009
London, United Kingdom, Planet Earth

CONTENTS

AUTHOR'S NOTE

THE DIVINE MOTHER SPEAKS through her heartfelt aspect: The Goddess Hathor. As we know, the Divine Mother takes on myriad forms, i.e., Durga, Laxmi, Venus, Mother Mary, Kwan Yin, and so many others.

Here the Goddess Hathor becomes the Divine Mother's sacred vehicle to deliver this profound message on heart healing for humanity.

— Channeled by Rashmi Khilnani

FOREWORD
By Leonard Orr

ENERGY BECOMES WHAT IT thinks about. This is the most basic truth about life.

If you really understand these words, you are spiritually enlightened.

Energy becomes what it thinks about. Energy is the Source of all things. Energy is Infinite Being, the Eternal Spirit; Energy is Substance. Energy is God. Love is also essential. Love is the subjective experience of Infinite Energy. To the extent that we feel love, we are tuned into our Divine Energy.

Energy and love is what this profound and beautiful book teaches on a deep level. As the founder of Rebirthing-Breathwork, I have devoted my life to learning about energy and love. Rebirthing-Breathwork, aka *Intuitive Energy Breathing* or *Conscious Energy Breathing*, is the ability to breathe Energy as well as air. Learning to breathe from the Breath Itself is eternal and never changes. Just as I teach that the lungs are the pathway to healing and the Divine, *The Goddess Hathor and the Healing of the Human Heart* reminds us that the heart is also a pathway to healing and the Divine. To love ourselves and be able to relate to others from our heart is a powerful practice.

The Goddess Hathor has channelled the material in this book through Rashmi Khilnani, healer, psychic intuitive, and creator of the *"Heart of Hathor"* Workshops. Rashmi teaches and practices several healing modalities including Sekhem, Seichim, Seichem, and Karuna® Reiki Mastery, and has taught Reiki Masters, doctors, scientists, and people from many walks of life the secrets of the Mystery School teachings. Rashmi also works and trains her Reiki Master students in the healing and rebalancing of the Sacred Elements and Mother Earth herself. Her healing sessions are powerful, as I can personally attest to, as can people from around the globe.

Rashmi and I are colleagues, fellow Babaji devotees, and good friends. She is a pioneer in energy medicine, working with twenty different energy modalities in addition to being a trained Rebirthing-Breathwork practitioner and teacher. She has warm generous goddess energy herself. It makes sense that Rashmi would be the channel for a book on energy healing and love. She is a very clear and powerful channel of the Divine Mother energies and Babaji, and is also a gifted healer.

The Divine Mother Speaks encompasses Rashmi's personal healing journey, including overcoming cancer and how it has been transformed through the heartfeltness and compassion of the Divine Mother Energies of the Mystery School of Hathor. Rashmi models what this book teaches.

This book brings to the earth at this time an updated translation of the ancient Universal Wisdom, particularly in relation to the Healing of the Human Heart and the alchemy of the union of the sacred archetypal male and female energies within and without. This includes the Five Elements that are the building blocks of our manifest universe, the difference between absolute and relative reality, the importance of feeling in healing, Sound, breath, and vibration, all archetypal energies of the universe for the conscious co-creation of our reality moment to moment.

It is particularly unique in that it has embraced and made simple the wisdom teachings of the universe and has graphically and clearly explained the difference between absolute and relative reality.

We can live in the transcendental state beyond the mind and freely choose, change, and manage our thoughts and our manifestations. This is our job as God's children. We can give and receive love and enjoy being supported by God. When we return to this through teachings and meditation—and heal our emotional mind, our mortal mind—our mastery expands and gets richer and more effortless. These are the rewards of being a spiritual seeker and pursuing spiritual growth.

Discovery is still going on for me as a spiritual seeker. Every year I learn more about breathing and spiritual liberation in very practical ways. Discovery must go on for all of us who seeking. This book is a must read for students of love, the heart, and spiritual realization.

I like that this ancient wisdom is presented by Rashmi in a contemporary work that enriches the heart and is available to people now.

I highly recommend you read it!

Truth, simplicity, and love,

Leonard Orr

INTRODUCTION
By Rashmi

WELCOME TO THE WONDROUS world of Goddess Hathor.

I believe that nothing in life is by chance. Something moved you to pick up this book. You have a deep knowing that you have been honored by doing so. Prepare yourself to receive a blessing of healing energy contained in these pages.

The Divine Mother Speaks brings in the energy of the Great Goddess Hathor, the Goddess of unconditional love, celebration, and joy—the Sky Goddess—the Fertility Goddess of the Mystery School of Ancient Egypt, with the view to healing your human heart. This archetypal energy, which came to Earth in the time of the Golden Ages in Egypt, is coming again in this challenging time for humanity here now.

The Goddess wants you to ask yourself these questions:

- Do you have trouble feeling your feelings?

- Do you wish for heaven on Earth?

- Would you like to have a deeper understanding of your beingness?

- Would you like a better relationship with significant others?

- Do you realize that healing is feeling?

- Do you wish to offload years of emotional baggage in hours, days, and weeks?

If your answer is yes, than you have been guided to the right source. *The Divine Mother Speaks* allows you to come to a deeper acceptance and love of yourself and others, and to have a deeper sense of peace and friendship with your heart.

The Divine Mother speaks powerfully, eloquently, and bestows an ocean of benediction and grace through this powerful yet simple material. The sacred marriage of the Divine Mother and Father energies and the application of Egyptian alchemy will balance and marry your male and female energies within and without. It will also balance the right and left hemispheres of the human brain, and the brain of Gaia herself will come into greater balance and groundedness, as you literally are becoming a body of light grounded on earth here, now, and in this amazing time to come.

Yes, your opportunity to know bliss is here. You can prepare for profound shifts that are occurring. Within your hands is the latest update on the change of frequencies leading up to 2012 and the ending of the Mayan calendar and help for you to come to a greater sense of grace and ease in this time of fast-changing paradigms.

This book contains an extensive in-depth simple understanding of Universal Life Force Energy in its multifaceted forms—the energy of love, the elements and the primordial energies of the universe made simple for you to use in becoming conscious co-creators in this time of bringing and becoming heaven on Earth.

Here are the wisdom teachings of all time made simple, the Egyptian Mystery School decoded and brought to your doorstep.

Energy is the key to the universe. You will learn many powerful and simple techniques to heal and stabilize in this time of colossal change—on Mother Earth and within all human beings. You will experience what took years and lifetimes of initiation and learning in the temples along the Nile in ancient times.

My name is Rashmi Khilnani and I work as a healer, energy master teacher, and channel all over the globe. Working with unseen beings, such as archangels, Sri 1008 Babaji, various aspects of the Divine Mother Energy and other ascended masters comes as second nature to me. If you feel that sounds seriously off the wall— I don't blame you!

Yet it is what happens.

In the many initiations that I conduct for Reiki Masters in different streams of Reiki that cover the wisdom teachings of all time, the Divine Mother comes through more and more strongly as the greatest catalyst in this Now Time as we move from the Age of Darkness to the Age of Light.

She has been whispering to me for quite a while now, to channel a workbook for emotional body healing and the strengthening of human hearts. While I was rushing around the planet using my gift as a psychic intuitive, I worked to facilitate in the awakening of as many people as I could to the higher frequencies of expanded consciousness through channeling Divine Mother Energies, and I was ignoring her call to write this book.

Finally being grounded in London over a few weeks to sell my Kensington Flat seemed to be a moment when the impulse was so strong, and I was shown the vision of this work in graphic detail in a state of lucid dreamtime.

I picked up the telephone and called my friend and colleague Amravati, and so we began. The book was to be finished within twenty-one days, which to my human mind seemed impossible. Looking back, it has been effortless and easy and the book has an energy of its own as the Divine Mother and Sri Babaji are really the force behind the words and who gets to be the editor, publisher, and so on.

As a heart specialist in my work as a metaphysical teacher and energy shaman, it seems natural that I have been chosen to be a channel for this work. My observation of my own life, and that of human beings all over the world, is that most of us have broken hearts and deep wounds of the heart, and the battle as to whether to continue to love or whether to give in to fear rages on. This is occurring in spite of the fact that the Photonic Energy of pure love is bombarding this planet to raise consciousness and increase the frequency of unconditional love in our run-up to 2012.

This book covers the esoteric wisdom not only of Ancient Egypt but also of other denominational wisdom within the embrace of Babaji's truth, love, and simplicity frequencies.

The mind will always hanker for complexity and methodology. Even a single sentence in this work—this sacred gift from the Divine Mother—can shift you exponentially.

My journey is here too. I wish to reach a high state of internal alchemy of my male and female energies, so that I can manifest deeper heartfelt loving relationships with myself, others, and the planet. Ignoring the current human dilemma and the challenges of Earth herself is no longer an option. It is crucial now for us to individually and collectively come to a greater state of balance and to facilitate in the rebalancing of Earth herself.

The heart is our epicenter—our deepest connection to our soul energy that is immortal and eternal. Through the balancing, healing, and the rejuvenating of our hearts and emotional states, we can reach heaven on Earth with effortless ease here and now. I trust that you will make the delightful discovery that the book is your friend and guide and effortless facilitator in achieving just that!

I am continuously challenged, processed, and healed through this work. The material is not for those who are unwilling to be courageous in facing their darkness, their fears, and their different emotional appetites.

This book is a request from Sri 1008 Babaji and the Goddess Hathor. It is being channeled at a rather challenging time of my life, as I leave the temple of my beloved studio in Kensington to journey forth as a global spiritual gypsy, to, I trust, continue to spread light, love, and the knowledge of universal life force energy all over the globe.

In the middle of uncertainty and half-packed boxes, my friend and colleague and fellow Babaji devotee Amravati and I met religiously against all sorts of odds. This book has an energy and life of its own and the Divine Mother and Father wished for it to be written now.

The amazing thing is that I channeled and Amravati courageously got everything down on the computer, periodically leaving her body and managing to get back down again. We found that whatever I channeled for the day intensely began to unfold in our lives (I am really having to walk my talk!).

The journey becomes more unknown, uncertain, and mysterious, but I know in my heart and I know my soul sister Amravati feels the same, as do many souls across the globe, that we are being guided, supported, and impulsed by our Goddess Nature to move forward step by step walking through fear and doubt into an expanded version of the light and love that we are.

I am grateful that the Goddess Hathor has used concepts, examples, and language that I as the channel understand and am familiar with. I feel very humbled to be given this task at this tumultuous time in human history. This book is not meant to be understood as a linear understanding. It is recommended that you open up in safety to your heartfelt feelings and responses, and use your knowingness in meditation if you choose to work with this material. Too much overcomplicated methodology of past or present spiritual practice has been omitted in this work in order to come to simplicity and effortless ease in the opening and healing of your hearts.

Take in this book slowly. The chapters are designed to let you savor them and use the information to integrate into your life. It is not to be read in one sitting, but instead to let the material grow inside of you so that you might flower.

My heart wishes your heart to heal so that it can soar to greater heights and allow you to feel heaven on Earth. The Goddess wants you to find the Divine within and without you.

Ladies and Gentlemen you are now on board flight 1008, the Hathor Love Express! Please fasten your seat belts, push back your love seats, and take a deep breath of bliss and ecstasy as you journey within to the magical space of your Heart!

Wishing you a pleasant Wings of Isis flight of being and becoming.

Love,

Rashmi

INTRODUCTION
By the Goddess Hathor

I, GODDESS HATHOR, AM here particularly to assist humanity with the safe opening, nurturing, and healing of the human heart. I am here currently from your past and your future to fill you with love, compassion, and heart wisdom. In ancient Egypt I impulsed many golden ages through my archetypal energy, unconditional love, creativity, ecstasy, joys, and celebration. Now I am here once again together with many other divine emanations of source, to assist in the strengthening of the Christ Grid, and to inspire you to bring heaven on Earth and move out of the age of slumber (Piscean Age) into the dawning of the Fifth-dimensional energies on Earth here now. Many evolved spiritual ascended species have converged into this sliver of time/space continuum to participate in the celestial party on planet Earth around 2012 AD.

The plan of the Divine Mother is for six billion human beings to wake up to a heartfelt state of Unity Consciousness (Christ Consciousness) at the end of the Mayan calendar and beyond.

Many of you have remembered me in this lifetime through joyful reconnection to ancient Egyptian temple art where I am depicted as the Divine Mother Cow or as the beautiful goddess with the horns of the cow enfolding the alchemy of Sun and Moon, male and female divine energy (which is an integration of the electromagnetic nature of this manifest universe).

Recently the excavations in Memphis have revealed another one of my magnificent ancient temples. The pillars of the temple in Memphis have beautifully preserved depictions of Hathor beings who very much work and teach the wisdom of the mystery school of Hathor. They work intimately with my archetypal energy in many dimensions (currently on Venus) to impulse love, compassion, and accelerated healing using sound, vibration, and ceremony.

I wish this book to be a gift to those of you who are courageously willing to now let go of struggle and victimhood and come into creating heaven on Earth and the expansive vistas of unconditional love and conscious co-creation. Therefore I will not be going in depth into those aspects of the ancient Egyptian teachings and terminology that are not relevant to moving into the new harmonic of expanded unconditional love and compassion in this glorious present time.

The reason that I choose to stick with current terminology and work with the spiritual energies of the moment is obvious. There is no point in regurgitating the frequencies of the last 13,000 years of the Age of Darkness or sleep—the Age of Pisces. This Age of Aquarius is dawning, expanding, and impulsing you to wake up to a full activation of your DNA from 2 helix to 12. The harmonics and frequencies of this age are facilitating the release of fight or flight, struggle, victimhood, blame and shame, and intense sacrifice (all Age of Piscean paradigms). The darkest hour comes before the dawn, therefore, currently, many of you are experiencing intense states of the above mentioned Piscean paradigms in order to hopefully experience them, get fully fed up with them, and then choose love, simplicity, harmony, and peace instead.

The Divine Mother Speaks

1

HEALING IS FEELING

IN THE ANCIENT EGYPTIAN Mystery Schools, I taught you about the emotional body and its connection to your spiritual body and ascension. All creation either evolves or devolves. You are once again in a cycle of the waking up of consciousness.

Therefore it is time to move forward, in love and trust. Come out of your little minds and heads into the realm of your heartfelt states of being. In other words, open the "Parachute of the Heart." Dealing with feeling, *your* feelings, is best done in a safe, preferably protected sacred space and with people and in places where you feel free to open up. All of Earth is sacred.

> **As you know, your attention + intention = manifestation**

Feeling your feelings requires balance, non judgment, and wisdom. By invoking the angels and ascended masters, you can allow your emotions (energies in motion) to be expressed and released safely and without the judgment of your mind. As you do this, you become more creative, light, and free to move and participate in life.

Awareness is key. Another word for awareness is consciousness. You are creating from your conscious, subconscious, and unconscious minds. To become aware of subconscious and unconscious states, it is essential to meditate, to chant, to be quiet, be in nature, to eat lighter foods, and to know that you know. A very powerful way to heal subconscious and unconscious unhealthy thoughts and patterns is through being initiated into the Reiki and SKHM systems. Another very powerful and simple way is to reprogram the unconscious and subconscious through connecting to a good hypnotherapist. *I cannot emphasize the importance of awareness in your life enough as you move through changing times, systems, and structures of your reality.*

Emotions like anger can be safely and appropriately released without causing harm to self and others through dancing, painting, writing, or even using a pillow. Unless you clear your emotional body and safely release suppressed and repressed emotions that you judge as being bad, there is no healing.

The word healing means "making whole and complete" as the wise Native American people knew. Everything in the universe goes in a circle. Your manifest reality is made of sacred spirals of energy. The seasons go in a circle and the planets orbit in a circle. In fact the illusion of the circle is a spiral with everything changing and either going upward or descending through the spirals.

In healing you are stepping onto an upward spiral with all obsolete (energies) being transmuted to the higher frequencies as you ascend. Nothing is ever destroyed, but merely transformed or rearranged. When we let go of thoughts, the energies holding the thoughts are transformed to new ideas and paradigms.

As the *Course In Miracles* says, everything is either love or fear, and fear is the absence of love. *Stress is nothing but fear. You, my children, have become attached to your stresses as an art form! However, you are beginning to realize the deadly effects of stress and tension to your mind, to your body, and to your spiritual being.*

As you understood in ancient lives in the temple of Isis, the Goddess is about Being. This is the time to become a Human Being and release your attachment to doing, rushing, and busy-ness. Healing is about Being. As the Bible says, "Be Still and Know." The word Pharaoh means "Being and Becoming." The pure Pharaohs of ancient Egypt were high level spiritual initiates who brought down to Earth this vibration of pure Beingness for humanity.

We will discuss fear in great depth in this book. It is only going through fear and coming out the other side into love that creates magic in your reality. Ultimately fear is an illusion and love cannot be destroyed. *The definition of fear is excitement out of time.* To release something you have to first understand it and feel it for a moment. Another way to understand fear is as an absence of love. It is time now to come out of the paradigm of "fight or flight" and embrace the new frequencies that are bombarding your reality.

Photonic Energy is different from protons, electrons, and neutrons. Photons are pure light beyond time and space. *Light is information and a bigger picture of the truth.*

It is therefore important now for you to question everything so that you can come out of your cozy cubby holes and the limitations of what you think is possible, into using greater and greater parts of your brain, including the right and left hemispheres. Your manifestations are becoming more and more instantaneous. Just to remind you, "As you sow, so shall you reap." *Why not choose Gardens of Eden?*

Healing is about taking responsibility and letting go of blame and shame. Remember that in your reality everything is a mirror. In Egypt we call it "the Mirror of Hathor." Instead of trying to fix the problem from the outside, go to the root (your inner reality) and examine how you feel, think, or perceive the issue.

Healing

Healing is definitely not about fixing others. As conscious healers it is important to remember not to force one's own agenda onto another's healing process. Sometimes the Mirror shows very traumatic or bizarre realities of the movies of our lives, but no matter how unacceptable the movie is on the mirror, if it is reflecting the screen of your life; *it is yours.* This may be a subconscious or unconscious co-creation that your mind is unaware of. Own your creations. *Breathe, feel, and then choose more consciously what you would like to see yourself attract and manifest into your life.*

THE ABSOLUTE AND THE RELATIVE

THIS BRINGS US TO *the subject of Absolute and Relative Reality.* In Absolute Reality, which you sometimes experience in meditation or when you become one with nature, all things are part of one energy, one consciousness; plants, trees, and individuals, "all that is", are one. (Unity consciousness.) In Relative Reality, there is polarity, separation, and on the personal creative side, individuality.

Absolute = all one
Relative = polarity, separation, individuality

A conscious human has the inner part of their awareness in Absolute Reality while the periphery or the personality is free to be individual and unique. This is wisdom. As we move into the fifth dimension and the frequencies of Christ Consciousness on this planet, the veils are thinning and you will feel less and less separate from others and your environment and nature.

It is so simple, this healing through seeing everything as the mirror of your own consciousness.

*So the Goddess wishes for you, as humanity now, to be consciously
co-creating heaven on Earth, whatever that means for you as an individual.* However, any creation that is ultimately not for a win-win
scenario and the highest-good-of-all-concerned is going to trigger karmic cause and effect. In fact it will create more and more
instant karma in these times when all on the planet is speeding up.

Absolute Reality

Remember, in Absolute Reality there is no time and space. This
is the fifth dimensional frequency that we are moving into in this
coming Age of Aquarius. So as per universal law, when your consciousness is in relative reality you must adhere to the universal laws
of time, space, and the third dimension. But as you move and get
grounded in absolute states of realty you become increasingly aware
of your inherent gifts such as clairaudience, telepathic communication, and clairvoyance. These gifts in Sanskrit are called *Siddhis*.

Absolute states of consciousness cannot be forced. Meditation is not about effort. It is the detached witnessing of the movies
and dramas of your life. The detached witnessing of your thoughts,
emotions, waking, sleeping, eating, walking states of being.

*As you know, energy flows where awareness goes. Thought cre-
ates your reality.* So becoming aware of your automatic thinking
processes is imperative if you wish to live in peace, flow, and love.
If you are always up in your head, (which most humans have a
tendency to be), the soft voice of your heart cannot really be heard
over the commotion.

3

SOUND, VIBRATION, POWER, AND TRANSFORMATION

So as you learned in that famous workshop in the 70s called EST, the mind is really like a machine, and to reactive as opposed to consciously spontaneous. The mind is there to doubt, think, and fear. It is useful, as a computer is useful, to create intellectually. However to have a computer on twenty-four hours of the day is stupidity. Your scientists know of the harmful effects of computers. Particularly for your children.

Through the sacred mystery school temples of ancient Egypt, I Goddess Hathor impulsed Golden Ages in Egypt. One of the most powerful alchemical secrets of the Egyptian Mystery School is connecting the heart to the different energy centers, i.e, connecting the heart to the throat for heartfelt communication (there you go, it is not a secret any more) or to the sacral center for sacred sex. Once you connect the heart to your mind, you can go into higher thinking, discernment as opposed to judgment, and opting for the higher-good-for-all-concerned as the preferred choice.

Just to clarify any confusion of the difference between judgment and discernment, we will bring in the teaching of Babaji, the Christ Yogi, who reminds us that within every sinner there is a saint, and within every saint, there is a sinner. Ultimately the Divine Mother does not judge us, as you have been wrongly taught in some of your religions. It is through making mistakes that you learn in the school of life; lifetime after lifetime. However, let it be noted that this does not mean that the universal law of cause and effect will not be triggered from your course of action. The more you move into All Love, Nonjudgment and into the Absolute State of Being in the here and now the less the laws of the relative will affect your reality. *You get to choose. Why not start experimenting now and see if it works?*

In the Age of Pisces, Jesus taught you of the power of forgiveness and the grace that comes from forgiving. *The grace that comes from forgiving can take you beyond cause and effect.* In the Age of Light, this grand wake-up cycle, a culmination of many lifetimes called the Age of Aquarius, this State of Grace is becoming increasingly available.

I encourage you to be expansive in your thinking and feeling to encompass the whole of humanity in your love and to honor and respect Mother Earth, as did the indigenous peoples. To think just of yourself, family, or country will no longer work. The Golden Web of life connects everything everywhere so it is a time to embrace this unity consciousness and make it part of your day-to-day awareness.

Sound

One of the most powerful keys of Hathor is the healing power of sound; both audible and inaudible sound. "First there was the word" and the word was sound. Then came the Light. Chanting, singing, playing devotional music to the Divine, and toning, are the easy way to opening the flower of the heart.

Making sounds of the things you wish to heal or shift such as a physical pain or a disturbing emotion, is also effective and simple in healing the symptoms. Unfortunately your mind and conditioning cause you to expect complexity as being all-powerful and the simple as being ineffective. More often than not, it is the other way around. Once you have released the pain, through making the sounds of that pain, you can make the sounds of peace or pleasure into that part of the body to recreate with sound as you wish. *Try it—it works.*

In all your sacred texts across the globe, you have read about the power of the sacred mantrams, the power in the name of the Divine: but still your mind keeps you from receiving the benediction of this simple practice. *Each day if you replace random thinking with the mantram like "om namaha shivaya," or "sa sekhem sahu," "Alleluliah," "Kodoish," "Adonai" or any name of the Divine of your choosing, you will become enlightened, heartfelt, and free.*

As you know, the universe means "the unity of verse." All of manifest reality is made of frequency, and each frequency has its own harmonic. *The law of resonance tells us that when a certain frequency vibrates, other cells of the same frequency will also begin to vibrate.* So the sound prompts the cells of the same frequency to vibrate and release congestion. The energy can then move freely through those cells as they are once again restored to their original harmonic. You are electromagnetic fields of energy. The Earth is an electromagnetic field of energy, so sound is a very powerful way to ground and to clear disease or congestion in your electromagnetic field. It is also a powerful way to time travel into the future or the past, particularly to the time of your ancestors.

I, the Divine Mother, am bringing in the energy of celebration. Your human hearts can heal deeply through celebration. *So I encourage you to come together in groups to dance your dance, sing your song, and regenerate Gaia with your drumming.*

Renewal

Your planet is making a loop of 13,000 years to realign with the time of Atlantis, a Golden Age. You are currently coming out of the chaos of a 13,000-year-cycle of sleep or darkness called Kali Yuga in the ancient Vedic texts. Ancient Hindi/Yogic texts define 13,000-year epochs as *Yugas*, noting that the years of Kali Yuga, is mankind's darkest hour.

As humanity, you have a chance to create or destroy. The wise aspect of destruction is letting go of the old for regeneration, rejuvenation, and the new; as the archetypal energies of Shiva and Sekmet demonstrate. This is the intention of destruction (or re-creation) of the pattern, to enable movement toward a higher perspective of consciousness and possibilities.

Ultimately Atlantis destroyed itself due to the overuse of the left hemisphere of the brain and by losing touch with Universal Law. This time, you again have a powerful opportunity to create. Are you going to choose creating instead to a higher harmonic, a higher paradigm? *It is up to you.*

The whole universe is here to help you choose creation this time. Your brothers and sisters from Higher Consciousness—the Pleidians, Sirians, and a whole host of other beings of light—are here to watch the show and inspire you to create out of the confusion a new vista of magnificent reality. *With your free will, what will you choose?*

Immortality

On the subject of immortality, I would like to remind you that matter cannot be created or destroyed, only rearranged. Therefore, energy can neither be created nor destroyed and dying is just about change and transformation. Many of you have incredible recall of past-life experiences. The ancient Egyptian Ankh (which is represented by the cross and a circle) is the symbol of immortality, and this knowledge and esoteric wisdom is being re-given to you for the time to come.

The cross in the Ankh signifies the four directions and the circle symbolizes eternity. What goes around comes around. Therefore, to meditate on the Ankh in your Third Eye or heart opens up the portals to the whole universe, which is within you.

The immortals that walk the Earth, such as Enoch, Babaji, and Mother Mary, are a shining example of what you are, and what you are becoming. But you cannot go into this state of eternity while wearing the comfy slippers of being conditioned into believing that you are limited to your current lifetime and there are forces that are beyond your control.

The subject of empowerment was given a lot of importance in the ancient temples along the Nile in my Egyptian Mystery School of Hathor. My aspect as the Goddess Sekmet explains this clearly. To be a true spiritual initiate requires a balance between spiritual power and humility.

> **It is important here to understand the difference between true humility and false humility.**

Spiritual power does not mean forcing others against their free will, no matter how righteous or beautiful the reality that you wish to enforce on another. They have their own perfect timing and development. However, inspiring or encouraging others on their spiritual journey, as you simultaneously work on your own, is not force. Balance is the key. Just as different mangoes on the same tree ripen in their own divine time and cannot be forced to ripen ahead of time, even for a delicious meal, different individuals have chosen the school of life for different lessons and we don't always know the bigger picture of their story. *When using spiritual power or healing energy, use your feeling body to help you, and always intend that the energy match the individual or group's agenda.*

Empowerment

Getting back to empowerment; your conditioning, which has taught you at times that you are not good enough, that you don't deserve, that you mustn't be an individual but always fit in the crowd, doesn't work anymore for a lot of you. To come into your own power with grace and humility is your birthright; to see the god or goddess within yourself and within all others is spiritual intelligence. Indians have a beautiful greeting: "Namaste," which means the god or goddess in me bows to the god or goddess in you. The Mayans understand the experience of "In Lakesh," which is "in you I see another me." Ultimately, to be truly empowered is to understand the law of

Unity Consciousness and as one learns to love and respect oneself as one is now, it is easier to love and respect others.

Meditation helps us to feel love for the self and leads to an overflow of this love for others as aspects of that supreme self. Spiritual power without open heartedness in appropriate situations leads to muddiness and stuck-ness. Ultimately the affirmation "as I prosper you, I prosper myself" is a wonderful paradigm.

> Run from any teacher who takes away your power. A good teacher will empower you and teach you to empower yourself and others, just as a candle's light is ignited by another candle.

A good teacher will also teach you ultimately to be independent of them at the right time. It is important to note that some of you think that to be spiritual is to give away your power to your spiritual teachers and to expect them to be in charge of you and responsible for your life. In the long term this does not work. Ultimately, no one is responsible for you except yourself, once you are an adult. It is good to use the guru (they who take us from the darkness to the light) as a ladder in your soul journey. It does not behoove you to be fixated on spiritual masters. It is no longer about becoming a Jesus or a Buddha.

The Creator's game is about becoming Yourself—being inspired by the great beings such as Jesus or Buddha is to see them as perfect Mirrors of Hathor in order to realize your own supreme being in your own unique way. This is the current game of the Creator. *You as gods or goddesses waking up can use your imagination to create your dreams into reality. Of course you also have full options to create your nightmares if you wish.*

The mind ego can be quite tricky for a spiritual aspirant. Ultimately everything is spiritual, including your mind. One of the favorite tricks your mind has to trip you up is to mix up the laws of Relative and Absolute Realities. An illustration of this is when we say, "Choose a wise teacher who empowers you"; your mind might trick you into the argument that the teacher doesn't empower you, that you empower yourself. Yes, this is correct in absolute reality, when there is no subject-object. But this holds true only for a fully realized being who is always in the now, moment-to-moment. In Relative Reality a good teacher's light will help to ignite you on your journey to self-empowerment.

4

BREATH

THE BREATH OF LIFE is something you often choose to ignore. *Humans have a tendency to repress and suppress their breath.* There are many reasons why you do this. *One of the great payoffs of holding your breath is it keeps you from feeling your feelings.* It keeps you in a more intellectual orientation. You feel that feeling your feelings will hurt you unbearably, but the truth is that not feeling your feelings causes disease and early death.

The in-breath takes in not just oxygen. With your intention you can also, with the in-breath, breathe in prana/reiki/chi. The out-breath breathes out carbon dioxide. I observe that most of you are exhale-orientated breathers and the goal of vitality and rejuvenation is to become an inhale-oriented breather.

> As you breathe more fully and deeply and trust and love your breath, you begin to love and trust your life more deeply also.

Breathing in nature (for example, by a large expanse of water), enhances your electromagnetic field of energy in a multitude of ways. Rebirthing, yogic breathing, and the Daoist practices are wonderful life-transforming and life-enhancing journeys on their own. The Rebirthing technique of learning conscious, connected, circular breathing gives you everything—success, youth, flow, connection, and love. The Rebirthing technique, if practiced with a good Rebirther and continued with personal training, enhances your connection to your mind, body, and spirit; to your negative and positive thoughts and emotions; and to past lives and to supreme bliss.

Your breath is a magical carpet on which you can journey into many dimensions and states of being. Every time you feel tense or stressed, overcome by emotion, or in a state of overwhelm in these challenging times of change: BREATHE. Breathe in to the discomfort, the disease, and the confusion. This helps the emotion (which is energy in motion) to move through the four-body system and release with ease.

> Your breath is a magical carpet on which you can journey into many dimensions and states of being.
>
> Every time you feel tense or stressed, overcome by emotion, or in a state of overwhelm in these challenging times of change:
>
> BREATHE.

5

INTEGRATION OF POLARITIES

YOU LIVE IN A REALM of duality and this brings us to a meditation on the polarities in your world—night and day, love and war, birth and death, hot and cold, male and female. Your beingness oscillates madly between these polarities, and peace goes out of the window.

> Your beingness oscillates madly between these polarities, and peace goes out of the window.

For a lot of you, the whole of your spiritual journey is to find ways to come out of the mind (which is moving from one polarity to the other), into a balance of opposites. All of the Vedas, the Kabbala, and Egyptian Alchemy of the School of Hathor give you the keys to integrate and move from duality into unity consciousness.

At this present time Earth and all its peoples have one foot in third-dimension polarity consciousness and are stepping more and more into the fifth dimension, which is beyond mind and division.

3-D = polarity consciousness

5-D = beyond mind, beyond division

One example of how the polarities operate in your realm is in the field of human emotions. One of your laws is that every time you feel one polarity of an emotion (such as love), the other polarity (hate) will pop up, so all that is less than love will come up for examination when you go into deep states of loving. You do, however, have full choice not to experience the 365-day Broadway hit of the undesirable aspect of the emotion. (In this case, hate or fear). Once an extreme polarity is reached, movement occurs back towards its opposite.

As humans, due to aeons of heartbreak and betrayal, you find it extremely difficult to trust the power of love in your hearts and to open up to others. If you become aware of this powerful law of polarities you will find it easier to open the petals of your heart in love to another or self because you will be fully expecting the other side of the coin to come up to say "hello." Forewarned is forearmed! You can ride the polarity and come back to the preferred choice, which is love.

Similarly, as you go more and more into the light on your spiritual journey, the dark will come up for examination. This was taught over aeons (the time span of ages), in the Egyptian temples. Now your initiations are happening moment-to-moment in your daily lives as time is speeding up and you are being encouraged to wake up quickly.

> Similarly, as you go more and more into the
> light on your spiritual journey, the
> dark will come up for examination.

Every time you light a large light you will experience a large shadow. Ultimately the shadow is not real but a trick of the light. Here I would also like to point out that the dark plays a vital role in this world to bring us back to the light.

As spiritual aspirants, I note with dismay that many of you feel you don't have a shadow at all. You feel "Holier than Thou." You feel like you are the Holy of Holies. And guess what?—you are, in absolute reality. However, a good analogy would be a mirror with dust on it. You are a pristine mirror of light on which the dust of the samskaras (the tendencies of many lifetimes, habits, and patterns) has landed. To clear this dust, simply take a feather duster of the light of your awareness, choose to come out of your head (which keeps you in the past or the future), and come into the power of the Now Moment. Then instead of acting in a reactive way based on the patterns of your lineage, your gender, your country, or any other past pattern, act authentically from the power of consciously choosing spontaneously in the Now. All the tyrants in your history taught you something, i.e., not to choose to create a disharmonious reality. The highest-good-of-all-concerned is not just a spiritual concept; it is also a practical choice to make. This is something you are beginning to realize, as you become more global and thanks to your Internet. Everything affects everyone everywhere!

Everything affects everyone everywhere!

A lot of your spiritual teachers choose to teach you about the light but ignore teaching you about the dark. The dark encompasses all that you are unaware of, unconscious of, and all that you repress and suppress. It also includes all that you judge to be bad or wrong or not allowed.

> **Anything that you deny will only become bigger: resistance equals persistence.**

The way to integrate the dark into the light of you is through becoming aware of your repressed and suppressed stuff. Healing repressed material, for example, by acknowledging it and then embracing it into the lightness of your being. *I observe that many of you are stuck in not realizing that you need to forgive yourself and then let go.* Come back to innocence. Contrary to what some of your religions have taught you, the Creator does not judge you for anything.

> **Forgive.**
> **Let Go.**
> **Come back to innocence.**

In each lifetime the soul chooses a different role to experience a myriad of realities through lifetimes, including so-called dark life times. The soul is like a movie screen—it is not ultimately born, does not die, cannot be made wet or be burned or killed. It is eternal and a direct emanation of source. The lifetimes are like movies on the screen of the soul.

Vibration is a very important aspect on the healing journey of the heart. Many of you wish to attract the ultimate romantic partners. If you have not learned to love yourself it is difficult to truly love another. As you vibrate at a higher frequency of self-love, self-forgiveness, and the honoring of the self; you begin to attract partners, friends, all types of relationship that match your vibration.

Very often, when you are feeling totally challenged in your relationships with your children, partners, parents, and others it is a perfect moment of mirroring of your own inner suppressed shadow. *At other times, your relationships are powerful tools mirroring the polarities you are needing most to integrate into your own personality in a given moment* (e.g., you, as a woman, might attract a very macho man into your life to help you to integrate your own very neglected male aspects). Also if you have an unhealed pattern of dysfunctional behavior, you will attract a mate to assist you to repeat that pattern until you have had enough of that particular type of drama and have taken steps to heal.

Just forgiving yourself is not going to trigger major transformation. *Forgiveness of your parents is very vital and frees up your energy to create a new paradigm that shifts you and heals your entire genetic line. A partial forgiveness of self, parents, and others will give you partial healing. Why not go for 100 percent?*

Forgiveness of your parents is very vital and frees up your energy to create a new paradigm that shifts you and heals your entire genetic line.

6

SEX AND RELATIONSHIP, FORGIVENESS, MANIFESTATION

I, GODDESS HATHOR, *am here to help you heal your very human heart. As you know, healing happens in layers.* Like the layers of an onion, you can deal with one layer at a time until there is nothing left of that issue to heal. The heart cannot be forced open. It requires an atmosphere of safety and protection. As your great mystic Osho says, the four keys to love and the safe opening of the heart are:

1. Be here now.

2. Be nothing.

3. Share everything.

4. When the shadow pops up, wait and if you wait long enough, as per universal law, you come back round the merry-go-round to feeling love again (*please refer to the work of Osho for more information*).

On the subject of being nothing, as we said before, false humility is not really being humble.

In love, there is a deep letting go and going into the void of the deep silence of the inner temple of yourself. In deep states of love, the personality totally dissolves—the state that is called "agape." This is why love is so scary for a lot of you. To be nothing, you have to be in a state of "no mind," releasing past and future. Ultimately, the heart is beyond time and space.

Sacred Sex, Another Opening of the Human Heart

A true practitioner of tantric yoga understands how to merge the human with the divine at the moment of ecstasy thereby making the experience of bliss multidimensional. In tantra, there is a deep surrendering to the god/goddess in the heart of the beloved and therefore a dissolving of the personality selves of the two individuals. The energy that is released through sacred sex is taken up through the chakras from the root to the crown and offered up to the Divine. The orgasm experience becomes a full-body experience not just a lower-chakra experience. As a tantric practitioner advances, there is a merging of the self with the whole universe. *The lovemaking is pure meditation as the two merge into one.*

There are different schools of tantra. In the Daoist school, the male is trained into mastery of withholding ejaculation. This is done in order to preserve the Chi energy. In Egyptian tantra, on the other hand, there is no withholding. There is a great emphasis on foreplay and nestling in the energies of the orgasmic experience.

In one school of Egyptian tantra there is a powerful practice called Ankhing. At the moment of ecstatic release and union, the energies are breathed up from root to throat and then looped around the spiritual chakras within the aura to connect with the divine.

As I have mentioned to you before, connecting your heart to your sacral and root chakras is a very powerful way to initiate sacred sex. It is also important to note that every time you engage in the sexual act with another there is a deep merging of electromagnetic energy and very often you take on a lot of your partner's stuff. A higher understanding of romantic love is not about how long it lasts but how authentically you are in heartfelt states moment-to-moment.

A lot of you are puzzled because you follow your conditioning on the subject of loving and then you don't get what your heart truly desires. Wisdom dictates letting go of preconceived ideas of fairytale love. *Begin to truly vibrate and practice the simple esoteric wisdom of being here now, being aware of your energy, and being authentic to the feeling of your heart, moment-to-moment.* The magnetic part of your electromagnetic field literally attracts or repels you from certain individuals. *I observe that very often you squash the uneasy feelings and get into a relationship with someone following your head and logic and reason as opposed to the soft whisperings of your heart. Many of you do this because it helps you to feel in control.*

Love is a child of freedom, and your soul and heart are seeking freedom at all times. This is the freedom to be who you truly are, which is not a name, a religion, a nationality, or so on, but an immortal soul here to experience creativity and joy through open-heartedness.

> Love is a child of freedom, and your soul and heart are seeking freedom at all times.

To open your heart in unsafe, un-nurturing environments will only lead to the flower of your heart closing up. *As you love yourself through vibration and the law of magnetic attraction you will attract partners who love and honor you as you respect and honor yourself. Once again the choice is yours.*

Breaking the habit of lifetimes is a challenge, but this is the crux of the game of life. *If you practice something with sincerity for twenty-one consecutive days you will be amazed at how you can break patterns and replace dysfunctional behavior with a brand-new floppy disc: the movie of your dreams.*

So many of you will say this is all very well but "I don't know what I want." "Am I not supposed to want what my parents want for me, what my country wants for me and so on?" Unless you make time to create space for silence, for non-doing, and for meditation to go within to the root of your being, you will never know who you are and what your heart wishes to create moment-to-moment. Human beings find it extremely difficult to be still. Unless the womb is empty there is no space for the baby to be conceived and created. So unless you allow for a space in your life, there is no real heartfelt creativity.

> Unless the womb is empty there is no space for the baby to be conceived and created. So unless you allow for a space in your life, there is no real heartfelt creativity.

Your mind can only exist in the past and the future. In the Now, it dissolves and you come into the space of your supreme being and becoming. Practicing the meditation technique of your great yogi, Ramana Maharishi, which is the "Who Am I?" meditation, is an *express route* to a state of No Mind.

Your mind and ego are important in relative reality as part of your unique individuality and freedom of will. *However it is prudent to realize that your soul, expressed through the voice of your heart, is the master of your essence and is the mainline socket to the divine. Are you going to choose to be a mere mortal or are you going to choose the option that is now being presented to you of becoming a multidimensional, immortal god/goddess?* Option A keeps you in limitation and control; and B, the second option, of becoming more of your god/goddess nature, is already within you and gives you access to limitless being.

Your imagination is a wondrous key to what you may choose to create and become. As long as your creations cover "win-win" scenarios, i.e., the highest good, you will move gracefully from miracle to miracle in your life. Synergy will become your second nature. Your manifestations will become more instantaneous.

Therefore to feel powerless and controlled by your parents, your government, your lack of finances, or love is no longer a paradigm that works. The Creator allows you to choose victimhood and powerlessness if that is what you truly wish for. It is your responsibility, as a god/goddess waking-up, to choose wisely. *As I have said before, time is speeding up and your life is a moment-to-moment intense initiation to help you wake up.* Many of you are having deep and spontaneous realizations of the consequences of left-hemispheric linear thinking. It is crucial that as Gaia wakes up to being whole-brained that humans keep up and match her frequency so that they have a greater balance in the use of the right and left hemispheres of their brains. There are many healing modalities in addition to meditation that help achieve this balance. Advanced Sound Wave Energy Therapy, for example, introduced to a scientist Reiki Master in Washington, DC, in 1995, achieves this state of brain balance more and more powerfully with each session.

It is interesting to see that many human beings that are attracted to their spiritual journey at this time of the Grand Awakening are wonderfully attached to their self-help books and these books are wonderful tools. *Ultimately, though, no matter how many spiritual books you read or how many spiritual seminars you attend, to become enlightened and a conscious co-creator of heaven-on-Earth requires you to do your own inner work.* It requires you to be willing to change. It requires you to be a courageous spiritual warrior and as a wondrous aspect of the Divine Father, Babaji says, to "think your own thoughts and be your own person." Spiritual entertainment, e.g., spiritual books and seminars, are wondrous and helpful in the healing of the human heart.

To truly heal your heart and become a Divine Human Being walking the earth now, the practice of meditation, (of becoming aware of your energy, your intentions, your pre-dispositions) is imperative. Balance is a key. Some of you are using your meditation to avoid living fully and passionately and sometimes to avoid feeling your feelings.

The time of sitting on the mountaintop or in caves to achieve enlightenment is no longer as relevant as in times gone by. As your holy books observe, (in this age of coming from darkness-to-light), attaining spiritual awareness and enlightenment through committed relationship is the most challenging path to choose. It is also the most rewarding.

Maya = Grand Illusion

In absolute reality there are no relationships. There are no subjects and objects; there is just the maya. There is just the Supreme Being one consciousness. In relative reality, (*well we know about that don't we?*)—you have a Mummy and a Daddy, possibly some children, and a man/woman that you love. So in Egyptian alchemy we use our relationship with others (1), our relationship with the sacred elements (2), our relationship with our karma yoga or our life work (3), and our relationship with our own inner supreme self (4), as the 4 corners of our pyramid to ascension.

Ascension

Perhaps you wonder what ascension is? Consciousness is always in a state of evolution. Your human body is literally becoming lighter. It is about bringing heaven to Earth, not spacing out. Earth herself is becoming lighter. To always stick with the intellectual rather than the experiential understanding of a concept is folly. You need to experience the taste of water to know what water is. To blindly follow what you read, what you see on television, and what your teachers tell you is no longer working well in this time of accelerated transformation. Experimentation and practice are important keys to understanding.

Many of you are suffering from a chronic state of boredom and an addiction to fast entertainment. Boredom is a disease of the mind. It is usually not at the root of the matter. At the root the issue may be one of victimhood, powerlessness, and/or a complete disconnection from your heart. Boredom is resistance to change. It could also be a resistance to the acceptance of what is in the present moment. Boredom is one of the foes of open-heartedness.

> Boredom is resistance to change.
> It could also be a resistance to the acceptance of what is in the present moment.

A most sensational and delightful way of connecting to your heart is through learning by observing the wondrous play of your children. Children are very strongly connected to their soul energy, and the divine open-heartedness, spontaneity, and authenticity to their feelings comes very naturally to them. As the Bible says, "Unless you become like little children you cannot enter the Kingdom of Heaven." Your heart is the portal to your kingdom of heaven, which is within you. By a return to simplicity and the wonder of the simple in your life, you strengthen your innocence and the love vibration of your aura is amazingly multiplied.

Humor

Here is another delightful and joyous key for you as you ride the tidal waves of change; at the same time being supported and surrounded by a state of spiritual impeccability and grace. My aspect as the cat goddess Bast signifies the importance of humor and joy in your lives. Very often and unfortunately, your education makes you more and more serious. A good yardstick for checking whether you are operating from your mind or heart is to observe how serious you are being in a particular moment.

It is fantastic when you begin to see the cosmic joke of Maya; the illusion of duality. *My channel Rashmi is always amused that some of her clients protest that she has helped them heal themselves with humor when they were expecting to be crying buckets in the session.*

The Divine emanation of All That Is, Krishna, is another delightful example of the healing power of play and laughter. He is often portrayed playing the flute, always smiling. Get into tickling each other if necessary! Laughter is the ultimate medicine as it encourages actual physical release of pent-up emotions and chemically releases endorphins. It is ridiculous that many of you feel guilty about playtime and laughter, which are precious moments to heal your inner child. The healing of your inner child is covered in most of the major modalities of healing on your planet. The inner child connects you to the goddess source within you. Your inner child also absorbs a lot of your pain, suffering, guilt, etc. So releasing the stored up issues of the inner child helps you to come back to your natural heart-felt states of being.

> The healing of your inner child is covered in most of the major modalities of healing on your planet.

A grand key of the School of Hathor to open up those hearts of yours (with their Fort Knox protection), is the conscious connection to your Higher Self; in esoteric wisdom sometimes called the "Fiduciary." For a lot of you, it is the case of your Higher Self going in one direction and your personality self (ego mind) very often walking the other way. This obviously leads you to feeling disintegrated, conflicted, and confused. *There is no possibility of knowing yourself without "Stillness" being a daily practice.* Another way to connect to the voice of your soul is through creative writing or journal keeping. Writing helps you to intimately connect to your thought processes, your emotions, and your aspirations in any given moment. As we have said before, intentionality and focus help you manifest your reality. Once you begin to realize the direction or tendencies of your personality and become acquainted with the agenda of your Higher Self, you can choose more consciously how to balance both. The integration of mind and heart was one of the primary goals of the Egyptian Mystery School.

The entire manifest reality that you experience in this universe comes from the unmanifest. This is something you find very difficult to comprehend. Most of you still feel that your reality happens from the outside to the within. This is not so. Pure potentiality of the unmanifest within you is the bedrock of your creation of the movies and dramas of your life. Everything you wish to know is within you. You have been told this time and again via the esoteric wisdom that you've encountered on your life's journey. The childhood song, "Row, row, row your boat gently down the stream; merrily, merrily, merrily, merrily, life is but a dream" encapsulates the essence of you as a conscious co-creator. So do you dare to dream the impossible dream? The destiny of mankind is beckoning you towards magnificent new vistas of possibility and magic.

> Most of you still feel that your reality happens from the outside to the within. This is not so.

Activate Manifestation

1. *Your heart and heart-felt passion are the triggers for this creative success.* Unless you have fueled your goals with passion and heartfelt energy, there will be no fuel in the engine of wise creation.

2. If the goal is just self-orientated, you create within a narrow spectrum. When you create with the good of mankind in your heart as the goal, you create from a much larger spectrum, and a much broader basis of possibilities and probabilities get triggered.

3. *Meditation is the express route to connecting with the void, the gap, the power of the unmanifest.* All states of no mind will take you to this sacred space as well. A peaceful time with nature is one example.

Some of the geniuses on your planet had full understanding of the magical law of unmanifest to manifest. When Einstein was stuck, he would pray, go into the void, and wait for the answer. Many of you don't trust your own intuition, your own information from within yourselves. You find it easier to take on the second-hand information from outside of yourself. The payoff of this dysfunctional behavior is that you are able to pin the responsibility for the result of your actions, or decisions, outside of yourself (blaming your government, your teachers, your parents).

> Many of you don't trust your own intuition, your own information from within yourselves.
>
> You find it easier to take on the second-hand information from outside of yourself.

I can hear you screaming inside your head with the question, how do I know the difference between the voice of my Higher Self and the incessant voices of my mind? The voice of your heart and soul speaks in very subtle soft whispers. When you know, you know, and you get a strong feeling of your knowingness within your body. As soon as you start analyzing and judging the intuitive information, the magic genie of the voice of your heart disappears back very quickly into the lamp. *If you really want to be a sincere student of your intuitive ability, you have to go step by step, with a feeling of safety, into the unmanifest through meditation, chanting, and initiation.* Each level, for example of Reiki, takes you to a more expanded level of your own consciousness. It takes focus and practice to build the skills at each stage that allow the fullness of the next step.

Sometimes people argue that they are all healers already. But just as you have your education systems of left hemispheric thinking and learning, the esoteric realm has different levels of initiation. It takes focus and practice to build the skills. To go straight from kindergarten to a PhD. is inappropriate. In a similar way, if all the psychic gifts are granted before the "clearing of the channel," there may be a misuse of power. This is why esoteric gifts are given to match the level of spiritual mastery of the initiate. An advanced spiritual initiate, for example, in the Temples of Hathor, had many challenging initiations to help them go through to clear fear, guilt, shame, limitation, and control. In this lifetime, all the wisdom teachings of all times are being given to you served up on a platter. This is a benefit of moving in to a Golden Age of Light. Light, as you know, is information, and many of you are waking up to the ancient memories of your lifetimes as spiritual initiates of many different schools of esoteric understanding. The time of secrets and lies is coming to an end. However as you know, the night is darkest before the dawn. The more you reawaken to the spiritual wisdom of your past, the easier it is to transform and surf the tidal waves of accelerated change.

7

THE ELEMENTS

THE KEY OF HATHOR that gives us a comprehension of our conscious connection to the sacred elements is a vital understanding. The sacred elements earth, water, fire, air, and ether are the building blocks of your manifest universe, of your world and of your bodies. The many different streams of ancient spiritual practice have revered these sacred elements.

THE ELEMENTS

These elements are the building blocks of the Universe. When we understand them we understand the Universe.

When we understand fire, we understand every flash of cognition, every spark of ignition, the flames of desire and consumption, and the gentle embers at the close of each cycle. We understand alchemy and transformation, heat and light and the brilliance of the stars.

When we understand water, we understand the depth of emotion, the turning of tides, the reflection of beauty, and the cycles of life—rain, underground stream, spring, river, ocean, evaporation, and on and on ... We resonate with every cell in our body, every plant, every animal. We know the joy of the first sip or bathing in moonlight.

When we understand air, we understand the gentle power of breath, the carrier of Chi, the force of the winds, the refreshment of the breeze. We understand the exchange of gases, the flight of the eagle, and the gentle caress of a baby's breath on our cheek. We understand the inspiration of life and the exhalation and letting go of that which no longer serves us but is food for the plants.

When we understand earth, we understand the existence through aeons of time, stability, nurture, and slow vibration. We connect with the fabulous root structures of trees, the ashes of fires, and the slow alchemy as metals and crystal are formed. We understand the joy of sowing seeds, growth, and harvest. We understand rotting and decay and the food cycle.

When we understand ether, we understand melting and flowing and we open to the finer qualities of life. We look out to the Universe, we receive telepathic messages. We understand the interconnectedness of All That Is.

—By Amravati

Balancing the Elements

Chanting the sacred names of the elements helps you to balance them within your own being and within nature. You can refer to ancient Sanskrit, Egyptian, Chinese, or Native American versions—they are all powerful and effective. Initiates of Vedantic wisdom through the ages effectively worshipped and conducted ceremonies in praise and gratitude to the Divinity of these sacred elements. Today, partly due to the discovery of electricity, you have lost your connection to the firmament, to the sun and moon and to the power of fire.

Fire

Fire connects to your spirit, your creative potential, your passion. *If your fire energy is out of balance you might find yourself exploding and detonating at the drop of a hat or on the other hand you might find yourself apathetic towards passion and co-creation.* As the ancients knew so well, when you sit individually or in groups by the fire, the Goddess of Fire acts as a giant vacuum cleaner—clearing and realigning all your energy vortices (chakras). In the ancient Hindu practice of Yagna or Havan, the mouth of the Goddess (which is the Fire) is offered ghee (rarefied butter), fruits, nuts, and flowers as a grand offering of praise and love. Sacred mantrams are chanted during this process. As a result of this energy vortex the atmosphere for miles around is cleared and the vibrations raised. Try it; as they have done to regenerate Brazilian forests—it works equally effectively on humans, animals, and plants.

In the Egyptian temples a fire was kept burning twenty-four hours a day. In modern time the Zoroastrians of Persia keep the fire burning day and night in their temples.

Water

The sacred element of water corresponds to your human emotional body. As you know, you are 70 percent water. *So use water consciously to purify your energy fields through conscious bathing, showering, and communing with the sacred element of the Goddess of Water, i.e., while swimming and floating in your rivers, streams, and the ocean.* Many of you, I have noted with amusement, meditate for hours, or chant for days, but think that bathing every day is optional. Bathing is more powerful than showering to purify and clean not only your physical body but also your aura and all the chakras. There is something about full-body immersion that shifts your consciousness to a state of deep peace and bliss. P. S.: Becoming a prune in the bath is optional!

The waning and waxing of the moon govern the ebbing and flowing of the tides. The waxing and waning of the moon also affect the water in your body and your emotions. So being aware and conscious of how powerfully the elements affect us in our lives on a daily basis is a powerful step in life mastery. By connecting consciously with the ocean, you not only energize your energy fields with negative ions and prana energy, you reconnect to the primordial essence of your being.

I note that you feel that you are drinking plenty of fresh clean water, but many of you are dehydrated. You can reprogram the water simply through your intention, or, for example, through the use of sacred geometry as do your Reiki practitioners all over the world.

Air–Breath

One of the techniques in rebirthing is to use a snorkel in the bathtub to breathe underwater for a prolonged period, done with supervision of an experienced rebirthing practitioner. *This connects you to the safety and warmth of the womb and also connects you more consciously to sensations, emotions, and thoughts that are ready to come up and be experienced and released.* You may also go into bliss states that may occur from the powerful use of two sacred elements at the same time, i.e., water (through immersion) and air (through powerful conscious connected snorkel breathing).

Your deepest connection to life is through your breath, for, as you know, if you stop breathing long enough your physical body will die (transform into something else). The Vedic wisdom talks extensively about the power and importance of your breath. *One of the very effective yogic practices is that of alternate nostril breathing.* This is a simple technique that any yoga teacher could teach you. It helps to clear the nadis (vial energy channels in the body originating at the nostrils). Modalities like Advanced Sound Wave Energy Therapy apply inaudible sound at the nostrils to help heal brain chemicals (neuropeptides and neurotransmitters). Scientists and psychologists understand the importance of these neurotransmitters and neuropeptides on your nervous system and your emotional bodies. As we have said before, when you breathe in air you are breathing in oxygen but also prana/chi/reiki (life-force energy). *Your breath has the power to heal all four bodies (physical, emotional, mental, and spiritual) in the most effective way to give you infinite energy and to take you instantaneously out of lethargic and apathetic states of being.* Athletes and dancers understand this well.

In this magnificent time, the winds of change, and more change, are sweeping your globe. So you can choose whether you want to sail with the wind or against it. For example, sitting in a beautiful still boat watching the dolphins jump around you in the ocean as the sea breeze, as the Divine breath of the Goddess, clears the cobwebs of negative thinking, stuck emotions, and past trauma.

Even little thunderstorms have a very powerful healing effect on the atmosphere. They clear morphogenic stress, fear, and negativity in an instantaneous flash of thunder and lightning. The wind and rain (the sacred elements of air and water) cleanse and purify the atmosphere for miles around the epicenter of the storm.

Let it be noted here, that if humanity (collectively and individually) does not responsibly clear its anger and other stuck emotions, this energy builds up morphogenically as a disease on an individual level and has to be cleaned out by nature. Nature's way of clearing may be a composite of the sacred elements through tsunamis, hurricanes, tornados, and the like. This is how nature (which is synonymous with the sacred elements) purifies the Earth and restores balance. *So it is prudent to choose tiny safe outbursts of your stormy energy/emotions as opposed to a huge build up of pent-up feelings.* Both for individuals and countries, expressing emotions like anger in safe, small ways can prevent massive earthquakes and the like.

Speaking as the goddess Hathor, I would like you to understand what your great channel Seth explained beautifully in his book, *The Nature of the Individual and the Theory of Mass Events*. Through Jane Roberts, his channel, this entity of light explains that often a whole group of souls agree, as part of their soul contract, to depart a particular incarnation in a way that serves all of mankind. This business of thinking that just because floods are occurring in Bangladesh, they are not affecting you in England, is faulty comprehension. *As I have said before, everything affects everything everywhere and all of life is connected as a golden web of consciousness. There is a bigger picture.* To judge the story line of a particular soul's journey through the observation of their tale in just one incarnation is a folly. As mentioned previously, the soul chooses a multitude of lifetimes to experience a multitude of realities including challenging and so called "undesirable" realities.

The ancients understood the power of the wind well. If you listen meditatively to the breeze, it will teach you many secrets. This requires you to slow down. That, you say, is not possible. *I will give you a little secret here—in these times of speeding up, the only way not to be giddy and feel like you are falling off the roller coaster of accelerated change is through setting aside time to SLOW DOWN.*

> I will give you a little secret here—in these times of speeding up, the only way not to be giddy and feel like you are falling off the roller coaster of accelerated change is through setting aside time to SLOW DOWN.

So how does the sacred element of air (your breath) help you to feel more openhearted? Every time you feel the stirring of love the lotus of your heart begins to open. Then up pops fear, the opposite, and you slam the brakes: closing the heart. The "brakes" in this case, are represented by the muscular contraction that creates the holding of your breath. *To reopen the heart you need to consciously start to breathe regularly again.*

Earth

The Sacred Element of Earth makes up the physical temple of your body, of your beautiful planet earth, and third-dimension reality. Gaia is a jewel in this universe; unique and beautiful. The pictures your astronauts have taken from outer space show you the truth of the matter. Earth is matter. Many of you are happy to be spiritual beings floating about but have a problem with being present and grounded in your physical body temple here now.

Grounding

I would like to talk to you about grounding and protection. True spiritual mastery in this time is about bringing heaven to Earth, of bringing down the cosmic energies into your unique physicality and grounding it. Being a space cadet New Age-type does not serve you. You cannot really consciously manifest, or become a true co-creator in physical reality without being grounded.

Sound is a powerful way to help ground. Your mighty trees teach you about sending the roots of energy deep into the center of Mother Earth, and your branches from your Crown Chakra to connect with the whole of the Cosmos. *The higher you wish to go*

towards heaven, the deeper your roots need to go into the Earth to cre-
ate balance and stability. In the powerful system of Egyptian Reiki
called Sekhem, practitioners or initiates connect the fifth-dimensional energy through the Crown Chakra to the heart, and down
from the Root Chakra to the center of Mother Earth. The energy
is then brought up from the center of the Earth through the Root
Chakra of the initiate, into the heart. For healing self or others, the
energy is redirected out of the hands or Third Eye or heart. All this is
done through the power of intention. (Energy flows where intention
goes.) The Sekhem energy is therefore a very grounded energy.

Many of your other healing modalities teach you about grounding and protection. The modality of body harmony and the myriad
forms of massage practiced around the globe are all wonderful ways
to connect to the sacred temple of your physicality and to become
grounded. Grounding means the conscious connection of your
body to the Earth beneath, and building a loving relationship with
the Sacred Element of Earth.

When you ground yourself as healers and spiritual initiates
on your journey to higher consciousness, it is very important to
become aware of energy: both your energy and the energy of others. *It is important to bring in the practice of grounding particularly*
when you are feeling chaotic, neurotic, and, in some cases, even psy-
chotic. This practice greatly helps to stabilize your mind and fluctuat-
ing emotions. To be grounded without protection is slightly missing
the boat.

I hear very often that you are confused about protection. Let's
clarify this matter a little bit. When you are in the state of Absolute Reality, where you have a conscious experiential awareness of
yourself as "All That Is Here Now," there is no subject/object and
therefore the question of protection does not come into the equa-
tion. However, in the relative reality states that most of you find
yourself in (most of the time, as you move towards lighter states

of Being, protection may be revelation. In the Egyptian Mystery schools of Hathor and other Egyptian esoteric systems, we use the invocation of Anubis for protection.

> "In the Egyptian Mystery schools of Hathor and other Egyptian esoteric systems, we use the invocation of Anubis for protection."

Anubis is the Keeper and Guardian of the Galactic Night and is the guardian of the journey from the dark to the light. Other ideas for protection:

- You can invoke the power and protection of Archangel Michael, the patron Archangel of Protection.

- You can use small bunches of sage around your neck or smudge yourself and the room, again with dried sage.

Gratitude

An attitude of gratitude brings miracles into your life; it is so simple. *Gratitude to the sacred element of Earth, i.e, for delicious food to eat, for the beauty of nature, for these magnificent bodies, and our flora and fauna; all are part of the reverence and purification of the sacred element of Earth*. The grounding that occurs by walking around in bare feet especially on grass and by hugging trees is powerful.

Conscious connection to The Sacred Element of Earth, through Sacred Sex, opens the magic door to your hearts in blissful and ecstatic ways.

As books such as *The Revenge of Gaia* and other scientific studies have clarified, dishonoring the Earth and ecology are causing havoc to your planet. The polar caps are melting and many of your animals are becoming extinct. Pollution caused through unconscious living, feeling, and thinking, stress the need to revert back to balanced ecological practices.

The purification of the Sacred Elements within and without helps greatly in restoring balance and reversing or transmuting the negative effects of global dimming and warming.

There is a lot of debate about what is good to eat as a spiritual aspirant and what is not. *To have a generalization for all of humanity on the subject of food is unwise. Each person is individual and may have unique nutritional needs to rebalance their health. I advise you to eat consciously, to bless your food, to bring in prayer and gratitude, and to share.* Ultimately the body can transmute even arsenic, as has been demonstrated by some yogis. (If you think you can, you can!) Your beliefs around food affect the way nutrition influences your health. Overall, eating lightly and avoiding processed food is recommended. *Food organically grown with love and cooked with love is more important than the huge debates on what is good and bad for us.*

Vegetables, fruit, salad, whole grains such as rye and oats, and nuts and seeds, greatly enhance your life-force energy and are easy to digest, when eaten raw or cooked lightly. The digestion of meat is not an easy process for your bodies. Meat is a highly concentrated, dense food. It also requires a large amount of resources to produce meat as opposed to vegetarian food. So there is a strain on your bodies and on Gaia. Those who cannot imagine being vegetarian, can always cut back on meat consumption to only a minimum. It is quiet appalling the way the animals are treated and killed. The vibrations of this trauma are partly consumed by you when you eat processed, factory-produced meat. Balance is once again the key. Being intuitive and listening to your body when you go shopping or preparing your food keeps you in alignment with what your body really requires to keep a nutritional balance. *On the subject of sugar, if you consume too much sugar it makes you more mentally oriented.* Small amounts of unprocessed sugar are fine.

Purification and the Earth Element

Fasting is a powerful way to purify the earth element in your make-up or constitution. Using intuition and wisdom on the length and type of fast you choose is important. If doing a juice fast, it is better to stick with vegetable juices as opposed to just having fruit juice. This is because vegetables alkalize the body. Sugar and meat cause acidic states. When disease occurs in the body there is a high level of acidity connected to it.

Ether

The primordial sound "OM" is an express route to connecting to the sacred Element of Ether. *Ether has the highest vibration of all* the Sacred Elements. *It is subtle and beyond definition*. It is beyond the normal comprehension of the mind. You come to this connection with Ether (or the subtle life-force energy that permeates all living matter), through the energy of devotion, meditation, initiation, and love. The comprehension of ether is beautifully described in the sacred texts, the Vedas. You come to an understanding of it through a negation of what it isn't. This is called Neti Neti in your sacred Buddhist texts. Neti Neti means "neither this nor that." *So Ether cannot be directly perceived through the five senses*. You cannot touch it, smell it, see it, or taste it.

When you are in a state of grace and are being bestowed with the Siddhis, then many have the experience of the taste of holy nectar dripping into the back of the throat during meditative or trance states. A true comprehension of Ether comes during high vibratory states of being in Sacred Space and Unity Consciousness or during Sacred Ritual such as Yagnas or through the grace of enlightened beings and mystics. This sort of experience takes you out of the third-dimension reality into the fifth-dimension and beyond. As the magnificent pearl of wisdom of a book the Bhagavad-Gita states: "You are not the field, (the field being the mind, body, and the intellect): You are *the Knower* of the field, (being the knower of the mind, body, and intellect)."

> **You are not the field**
> **You are the knower of the field**
> **—Bhagavad-Gita**

In Sanskrit "the Knower" or the detached witness is called the "Sakshi." *The strengthening of the detached witnessing aspect of your consciousness is a key to feeling safe to open your heart.*

Ultimately, the Sacred Element of Ether is understood through your "knowingness" and takes you into expanded consciousness and the experience of the Unity of all living and nonliving matter. *Ether is not about definition, because whatever you define, you limit; it is experiential and beyond limitation.*

During initiations to the higher levels of Sekhem and Hathor Mystery Schools, initiates connect strongly to this Sacred Ether through Sacred Geometry, such as the portal symbols using Pyramid, Ankh, Lotus, and Infinity.

P. S.: In the Mystery School of Hathor, Ether continues to be an ongoing mystery. (joke)

The Sacred Elements are actual expanded entities of light and love that have given of themselves for the creation of your third-dimension reality. So praise and gratitude and conscious connection to them leads to conscious living and loving. As you love them as the building blocks of your reality, you go to the source of what you are made of and learn to love yourselves and your world, with the eyes of wonderment as a child of the universe.

8

QUALITIES OF
HEART-CENTEREDNESS

I'D LIKE TO TALK to you about how the universe operates: It operates through the laws of paradox and humor. It is very funny to note that every time one of your scientists does an experiment to prove something, another one of your scientists conducts a successful experiment proving the direct opposite. *The universe is very sympathetic to your intentions.* So if your intention is that oranges are good for you, the universe will rearrange itself to give you oranges that are good for you. Or the opposite, as the case may be.

Therefore, as you move into the fifth, impeccability of intention is important. Otherwise you land up manifesting your negative thoughts and expectations, more and more instantaneously as we move into 2012 and beyond. *The universe is paradoxical vis-à-vis third-dimensional reality because third-dimensional reality operates on the principal of duality (polarity).* Therefore, everything that occurs in your world has an equal and opposite energy that pops up to fulfill the polarity law.

Your third-dimensional reality operates on the law of humor as it mesmerizes you into the collective belief that you are solid and that your world is fixed and limited and very real. The truth is that your worldly reality is holographic—what your ancients called "Maya" or the Grand Illusion. Yes, in relative reality, if you cut your finger with a knife accidentally, your finger will bleed. However, on the screen of your soul, which is eternal and beyond the hologram, "no thing" is happening. The soul is not cutting or bleeding, it is a direct emanation of source—it is pure potentiality, it is beyond life and death. The soul is your best friend and in spite of its very detached nature, loves you dearly and intimately feels your pleasure and pain.

As mentioned before, this book is not to be taken literally. To mix the laws of the relative and the absolute in unwise combinations without the supervision of an enlightened master or teacher is dangerous. The Divine Mother is pouring out the wisdom teachings of all time to facilitate your accelerated waking up. *The use of metaphysical wisdom is best done slowly and with spiritual guidance, and balance.* If you can but see the joke and the sense of play as your talented entity Shakespeare said "all the world is a stage . . ." and you are playing your role.

Your sense of humor will serve you greatly in this magnificent time of the ending to time and instant manifestation. Deep belly laughing is recommended. Instead of going into the usual states of blame, shame, and victimhood, you can see the funny side of things if you so choose and *lighten up.*

In the Egyptian Cartouche, one invokes the energy of Bast, the cat goddess of play and laughter, to shift into the energy of humor with ease and grace. Ceremonial dancing and play were an intrinsic part of ancient Egyptian culture. Your heart resonates strongly to the frequency of humor and play. This is why some of you chase humorous mates like a heat-seeking missile.

The Heart does not see things as black and white. It somehow, when vibrating at its higher harmonics, transcends polarity consciousness. This is because the power of love is about integration and transcendence of the polarities and the power of love is capable of forgiving and transcending judgment. The mind on the other hand is obsessed with definition and analysis. As I have said before, as soon as we define something we limit it to that particular definition. So when you are loving with your mind as the boss, you are on a sticky wicket and an endless roller coaster of duality, e.g., I love/ I hate; I am happy/ I am unhappy; I want/ I don't want. To be heartfelt and allow the heart to be the boss is to strengthen and cultivate the vibrations of embracement, acceptance and compassion.

You cannot imagine how beloved you are to the divine Mother. What precious little jewels you are and the luminosity that you are stepping into. Every time you connect to the Divine Mother in your heart she answers your call immediately. I, the Goddess Hathor, am a very heartfelt aspect of the Divine Mother Isis, so by invoking me you get to go to heartfelt states with joy and ease. The qualities of compassion, embracement, and acceptance are all important for the healing of the human heart.

Compassion

Let's start with compassion. The enlightened Architurean being Buddha has taught you most beautifully about the art of compassion. Buddhists practice the intention of becoming enlightened and then being reborn to help others until the goal is reached: the freeing of all souls from the Maya (relative reality). Opening the thousand-petal lotus of the heart through breathing in heaven and Earth is a powerful way to connect to the compassion of your heart. This is a state that in some of your Buddhist texts is called "mahakaruna." Compassion is closer to empathy and is not the same as sympathy or "pitying others." *I note that many of you as healers and metaphysical teachers continue not to honor the distinction between compassion, which empowers all concerned, and pitying or imbalanced sympathy that tends to disempower others. I am not saying that sympathy in and of itself is an undesirable quality. It is a WONDERFUL STEP on the journey to the heart and to compassion.*

What is compassion? It is a deep experiential state of honoring the other as one honors oneself at the same time. It is much closer to feeling a deep empathy for the pain and suffering of another aspect of the one supreme self. *As you empathize with another's pain, it is prudent to continue to keep a part of your consciousness of yourself as a whole and well individual.* This does not mean that you have to be totally perfect before you begin to facilitate the healing journey of another or teach others that which you have learned through your experience. What is important is that during the healing session you put your energy largely in the Absolute where all is one and all is love and all is peace. This assists the recipient of the healing session to kick in to their own inner expanded consciousness, which helps them to immediately see their dramas and pain from a higher perspective.

Compassion is also your passion to which has been added love. In this state of compassion or "co-passion," it is so much easier to honor the passion of another. P. S.: Do not forget that we first start with compassion for ourselves.

This brings me to the subject of the sacred geometrical symbol used extensively in Egyptian Alchemy—the Divine Infinity Symbol, which is like a number eight on its side. *Love loves to journey through infinity.* So by meditating on the infinity symbol in your heart or third eye, you connect powerfully to the love of self as one loop of the infinity and the love of others as the second loop. This is a powerful Key of Hathor that has been used for eons for enlightenment, healing and triggering of loving, compassionate states of being.

Love loves to journey through infinity.

The Infinity Symbol symbolizes that you are eternal, that life is eternal, and like the Ankh, it symbolizes and reflects your immortal essence. It also illustrates beautifully that *what goes around comes around*. So based on this universal law of how energy moves in your universe, if you wish for love, become love. If you wish for peace, become peace. *The School of Hathor always takes you back to the source of your power which is within you.* So does every single spiritual path on your planet—Celtic, Sufi, Vedantic, Zen, and so on.

Embracement

The quality of embracement is another express route to unconditional love and the opening of the heart. Your human heart cannot be forced open. *The more you or the other uses pressure and guile to open the heart, the faster the heart closes its petals.* Love is a child of mystery. It requires safety and a feeling of being nourished and honored. So a daily practice of finding ways to listen to the desire for the well-being of your heart is recommended. Sometimes before you can hear your heart's voice, you need to clear emotions that may be coming up, such as anger or pain. *This is always to be done without causing further harm to self or others.*

Many of you, such as my channel Rashmi, have had an intense experience of the emotional body in my temples in Egypt even in current time. Her emotional body was highly activated, particularly around the solar plexus and heart, after meditating with a spiritual group in my temple in Dendara. What she experienced was all her emotions at the same time and a total opening of her heart. The morphogenic energy of love of my temple also cleared out a lot of the fear and imbalance of power in her solar plexus.

One of the powerful ways to integrate experiences such as the one described above and the intense pull and push of your emotions, thoughts, and life is through embracement. *Embracement means a total allowance and a total acceptance of what is.* This includes an embracement or allowance of your judgments and your so-called "lack of perfection." The Divine Mother sees you as a pristine jewel of perfection even within your imperfections.

Your saint of love, Amaji, illustrates the embracement principle both metaphysically and actually, when she transmits the love of the Divine Mother through hugging countless human beings on a daily basis. She offers love as the Divine Mother does . . . without judgment.

Acceptance

Together with compassion and embracement I would like to bring into your bouquet the flowers of acceptance. Acceptance and embracement are very close to each other. *In many of the biographies of your saints and enlightened Yogis, time and again they share with you the power of acceptance on the spiritual path.* The more readily you are willing to give up, through practice, your expectations and pre-conceived ideas and to come into the spontaneity of acting, rather than reacting, from the power of your Now Moment, the more immediately you access the magic zone of acceptance.

Meditation, chanting, toning, and reading the great scriptures such as the Shiva Purana or the *Book of Thoth*, and also modern channeled information such as *The Keys of Enoch* and *The Pleaiedean Agenda* and other high energy books all help to teach and inspire you into the principle of acceptance. Let go of the human tendency, to resist your heart's desire for acceptance of all that is. Purification of your mind through the sacred mantram, "Om Namah Shivaya" helps greatly to still the mind and bring you to the space of accepting your life as it unfolds moment-to-moment. "Om Namah Shivaya" simply means *I love myself, I honor myself, God/Goddess dwell within me as me.* Another meaning of this mahamantra (maha: great) is, *I seek refuge at the feet of the God/Goddess within my heart.* There are many other meanings to this deep magical tool of mind purification. *The aspect of the Divine Simple Father, Bhole Baba, who many of you know as Babaji, has stressed the importance of chanting this mantra to facilitate moving from Kali Yuga to Satha Yuga (moving from the Age of Pisces to the Age of Aquarius).* For those of you who chant this or other powerful mantrams as part of your daily practice of coming out of incessant thinking, acceptance comes naturally and easily.

The sacred mantram used in ancient Egypt and in current time by Sekhem initiates all over the world is, as we mentioned before, "Sa Sekhem Sahu." "Sa" is *the breath of life,* "Sekhem" means *spiritual power balanced with humility,* and "Sahu" means *the Realized Being and Becoming.*

One of the most perplexing aspects of human love that many of you find yourself in, is that the more deeply you love another, the greater is the capacity to "hurt" another or be hurt by the beloved. The most difficult relationship and the strongest loving bond in human terms starts with your earthly mother—she who conceived you and gave you birth. Many of you have chosen very challenging relationships with your earthly mothers in this current lifetime— this time for merging and clearing of past karma. As we have said before, the law of karma only operates in relative reality. The truth of the matter is that many of you will choose from your heart to love and honor your families and yet to walk on a completely different path from your family and ancestors at this time. *I, the Goddess, feel your pain. I feel your courage. For to choose from the heart requires you to be very brave and single-pointed on your spiritual journey. Finding the balance between honoring your parents and yet coming out into your own integrity is a wonderful forum for learning and growing. It is also where a lot of the pain is stuck in your hearts. Give me your pain, give me your suffering, and give me your anger. I will transmute it for you.*

The Divine Mother, we will call her Isis here (she has many names), can take you and your emotional baggage to a higher harmonic and transmute it. *This alchemy is based on the Law that if a problem or stuckness exists on one dimension, by going up a dimension or a couple of dimensions, you transcend the difficulty and come to a higher, more enlightened perspective.* Just to give you a picture for your mind, the panoramic view from a penthouse on Central Park is more expansive than one from the third floor of the same building. The perspective, by shifting position, changes your attitudinal view completely. At times, you will choose to give your pain and unresolved problems to an aspect of the Divine Father instead. In the Egyptian pantheon, we have many aspects to this holy energy . . . a very powerful one being the Divine Father, Ra. Equally effective would be Babaji, the simple father, Buddha, Jesus, or any other aspect of the Divine Male.

Unless you consciously begin to heal over time, layer by layer, the connection of the primordial relationships to your earthly mother and father, they come up in the unresolved issues that are regurgitated in your relationships—until healed. That is why, although changing partners may be a joyous choice, to use it as an escape from your mother/father issues does not work.

Most of you did not have the perfect atmosphere for the flourishing of Divine Love at the time of your birth. This is a given. After the initial shock and trauma of popping out of the safety and love of the womb, where everything was done for you, you go through childhood being this little person, with these towering adults probably bossing you around with their "shoulds" and "oughts" and "can'ts." Therein begins the grand struggle between the wonderment and magic of your soul connection, each year becoming dimmer, while the controlling adult perspective kicks in.

Untangling the knotted and convoluted memories and traumas (not the happy ones of course), particularly of the first ten years of your life, is crucial. *All this sounds like a lot of hard work and so many of you say "why bother?"* It is easier for me to "stay in my mind" and the illusion that "I get to control my reality." Deeply connected to this issue is also the human tendency to fix others, control other's behavior instead of working on shifting one's own attitudes and reactive behavior. This is all a part of the wonderful stormy challenging glorious path back to the magic mystery of your hearts. The only person you have the right to change and the full power to change is yourself. Others can be cajoled, tantalized, persuaded, inspired, or on the negative side, manipulated into change. *Manipulation and control of the behavior of others, especially your nearest and dearest, leads to the same consequences being inflicted upon you.* If you can come to the simple realization of honoring yourself and honoring others and honoring the differences between you, even if you don't agree with them, you come to a State of Grace; the alchemy of the heart. *If you wish for freedom and a release from limitation, control, and manipulation, the first step towards freedom is the allowance of granting this freedom to your parents, your children, and your beloved.*

At times, the consequences of following your heart involve greater and greater detachment from the people you love who are not journeying on the same pathway—frequency of the heart. This is of course extremely challenging and at times traumatic for many of you. In the ancient Egyptian Mystery School, spiritual initiates were put through many difficult tests on finding the balance between loving and detachment and also many initiations in the integration of higher mind and heart. Today the incompletions of past lives are coming up for each of you in quick succession to embrace, feel, heal, and release.

Discussing your dramas endlessly with each other is counterproductive as each of you is going through an accelerated amount of processing of lifetimes yourselves. Herein comes a balance between the wisdom of sharing and moving through your stuff and letting go. Let it be noted here, that as you heal an issue in a Now Moment, all past-life issues connected to that are usually simultaneously healed so an over-obsession with past-life regression is not required. On the other hand, at times, based on intuition, it is quite relevant to try and heal an issue coming up in the Now, that seems irresolvable, by going back into its root in another lifetime. An issue will not come up in this lifetime to be healed if it has already been healed and resolved in past lives.

An over obsession with the past takes you out of the power of the Now Moment. To be fully enlightened means to be fully present to the power of the Now, moment-to-moment. An enlightened being has no attachment to the illusion of their past or their future. They give themselves the present of their presence in the present. As we have said before, it is the mind that takes us into the past and future and keeps us fixated in duality, relative reality.

> An enlightened being has no attachment to the illusion of their past or their future.
>
> They give themselves the present of their presence in the present.

Cellular memory release, for example of past trauma or suffering, occurs from the DNA. But for this to be effective, your intention and a good healer are enough. Getting enamored by the various story lines of past lives and not going to the crux of the issue to be resolved is missing the point of past-life healing. *I do understand though, that it can be fantastic spiritual entertainment.*

9

ARCHETYPAL ENERGIES OF THE UNIVERSE

LET'S MOVE ON TO one of the most powerful and easy keys of Hathor in the healing of your magnificent human heart. This is the invocation of the archetypal energies of the universe depending on the issue on hand. In the Egyptian pantheon there are twenty-four main energies that Egyptian Alchemy uses for transmutation and healing. These are the four elements—Earth, Water, Fire, Air; nine of the Neters (gods/goddesses of ancient Egypt)—Isis, Nepthys, Hathor, Bast, Osiris, Horus, Ptah, Thoth, and Anubis; and the Sacred Archetypal Symbols—the Lotus, Scarab, the Pyramid, Sirius, the Crook and Flail, the Uraeus, the Sphinx, the Ankh, the Buckle of Isis, the Winged Disc, and the Sacred twins Tefnut and Shu. (Murray Hope in *The Egyptian Cartouche*, utilizes these).

I have discussed the invocation, use, and power of the Sacred Elements earlier in this book. The exciting thing about the use of archetypal energies in your life is that you can invoke them anywhere, anytime, at the drop of a hat. Of course, it would be wonderful for you to sit for hours by a beautiful fire in nature and purify and be inspired. However this is not always possible. Once you understand the magic of the archetypal energies, you could invoke the energy of fire within you immediately for inspiration, say for example during a business meeting.

You would like perhaps to understand more deeply the meaning of "archetypal." In the beginning of creation the creator used various energies to paint the universe and make it happen. These are the first or primordial energies—the first patterns of energy that were the building blocks of your known universe. So by tapping in to these energies through intention and attention you can strengthen these qualities within yourself and they work equally effectively on plants and animals. *Another example here would be if you are struggling with money issues you could invoke the "Element of Earth" to help you to come into greater abundant flow. To manifest anything in your third-dimensional reality on Earth, as I have mentioned before, you need to connect to Earth and ground. Money is part of your physical reality. I assure you that us Neters do not have to deal with mortgages and bank accounts!*

As many of you are having greater and greater past-life recall of ancient Egyptian lifetimes, the using of these ancient archetypal energies that many of you are familiar with will come easily and effortlessly to you. These archetypal energies can be easily converted into the ancient Indian, Tibetan, Chinese, Greek pantheons and so on. Experiment and see what works for you.

I, Goddess Hathor, would like to share the simple connection with nine of the many Neters of Egypt and highlight the archetypal energy that they symbolize. You then can go off and work with these energies very powerfully to heal your hearts and minds, if you so wish. It is important to have the attitude of reverence and praise to these energies when we invoke them. This increases the connection to these powerful frequencies. The greater your open-heartedness and feeling of sacredness, the greater is the benediction received and imbibed in your being.

The Nine Neters

Isis

When you invoke the Goddess Isis or meditate on her energy, you connect very strongly and quickly to your "is-ness" and to your Being. She is an all-encompassing, primordial, magnificent aspect of the Divine Mother. As you connect strongly with Her in your heart, she can help heal your mother issues and your issues of being a human being. She assists you in bringing the energy of the Divine Feminine into the four-body system of your Being. *I, Goddess Hathor, am the heartfelt aspect of Isis. Ultimately, we are One.* All the other feminine Neters such as Bast and Nepthysis come out of the womb of Isis. It is important to remember when invoking the Neters and other archetypal energies that although they may be symbolized by Goddesses in bodies and epitomized in statues and art all over Egypt, they are actually vast, mentally incomprehensible force fields of energy.

During high states of meditation and initiation, they do however sometimes bestow us with the grace of their presence as actual Beings. At times they have walked the Earth in human bodies. When we invoke the Neters, the unique frequency of that particular force field and pattern of energy may be activated without the appearance of a "human" form of the Neter, which is recognizable. The initiates of the Egyptian Mystery School understood this well. They also understood that ultimately any aspect of the Divine archetypal is an ongoing mystery and journey or revelation and enlightenment. *This is why I call it a Mystery School.* To intellectually comprehend the Keys of Hathor, the magic of alchemy, or the essence of any aspect of Divine Emanation is impossible and not recommended. However you may use your mind and intellectual understanding as a starting point from which you will later jump off into an actual experience of the unknown. In my Divine teaching to humans I very much stress the need for experiential understanding.

> To intellectually comprehend the Keys of Hathor, the magic of alchemy, or the essence of any aspect of Divine Emanation is impossible and not recommended.

Goddess Isis connects you strongly to the energies of compassion, caring, nurturing, and perseverance.

Nephthys

Invocation and working with the energies of the Sacred Neter Nephthys takes you into the void immediately and into the mystery of the unmanifest. She is oftentimes depicted in hieroglyphics with her hands raised in the manner of a Sacred Chalice. The deeper meditation and understanding of these powerful Sacred Egyptian mudras (body postures) was an intrinsic part of the curriculum of dance and sacred ritual in my temples along the Nile through eons. When corruption set in and the high priests and priestesses of ancient Egypt began a declining cycle, the sacred energies of the fifth-dimension (represented by Sirius) were cut-off at a level of declining purity. Akhneton and Neferti brought down the energies for a powerful strengthening of the Christ Grid on your planet hundreds of years before Jesus, who came later and continued the work of strengthening Christ Consciousness and the Grid. What Akhneton was really teaching the peoples of Egypt was Unity Consciousness. This made him very unpopular with the priests and priestesses of the time. The reason they were able to get rid of him was that he got caught up in the judgment of good and bad spiritual and nonspiritual. He fought the fight against the dark, forgetting that the Divine does not get caught up in the illusion of duality. At some point he forgot that he was there to transcend duality and to teach unity beyond the pairs of opposites. By falling into the trap of judgment his channel no longer met the sacred law of purity required for Unity Consciousness. The connection with Sirius through the great pyramid of Ghiza was disconnected by the spiritual hierarchies.

I, Goddess Hathor, would like to inform you that as the photonic energy called the Photon Belt is impulsing humanity and Mother Earth, in this time of now, the Sirus Connection is re-strengthening in Egypt and all over your planet.

Sacred wisdom was taken at the time of the decline of Atlantis to the Egyptian temples and this sacred wisdom was given and carried forward by the Essenes. As many of you know Jesus was an Essene.

For the last two thousand years humanity has been controlled by a very male aspect of the Divine and the Goddess, particularly in the western world.

Invocation of the archetypal energy of Nephthys connects you to that which is seemingly unknowable, i.e., things hidden. She can open you up to the knowledge for enlightenment. She connects you strongly to the energy of emptying to receive. She has the magical power to bestow the pearls of mysticism, peace, and other psychic gifts.

Hathor

I, Goddess Hathor, am symbolized throughout Egypt by the sacred horns within which is contained the Sun and the Moon (energies). This denotes the alchemy of male and female—the integration of the polarities. As I have mentioned previously, you are electromagnetic fields of energy. The Sun denotes the electrical or male aspect of each human being's energy field. The Moon symbolizes the female aspect, the magnetic component to your electromagnetic field. A very large part of the curriculum of the school of Hathor was the study of Egyptian alchemy, the marriage of Moon and Sun, Yin and Yang, within each initiate. As you know, each of you has a male and female part to your makeup. As you find the balance between these two polarities within your being, you become "whole and complete" and the heart is ready to open, receive, and give love to another "whole and complete" aspect of Self. There is, in other words, a mirroring on the outside of the state of being of your inner temple. As you know, the male energy within you of the Sun is electrical, it is dynamic and it's about doing, manifesting, and making things happen.

The feminine Moon energy within each of you corresponds to your Goddess nature, which is about being, allowing, accepting, embracing, and is the vital creative force of the universe. For eons on your planet you have been very dominated by the male energies and the Goddess frequency has taken a back seat. Even your women in modern times have become more and more male in their orientation. So as you come to balance your doingness with your beingness, and you ground yourself to the center of the planet, your heart is more easily able to open its thousand-petal lotus of unconditional love and embracement.

In ancient Egypt I, Goddess Hathor, was also symbolized by the divine sacred cow, my horns forming a holy chalice above my cow mother head. I was referred to as the Goddess of unconditional love, sacred sound, creativity, celebration, and fertility in different periods of ancient Egyptian history. Often times I was revered as the Sky Goddess of Egypt. When you invoke my archetypal energy you can connect to any or all of these qualities strongly and gracefully.

The Divine Mother is impulsing you to open your hearts and bring heaven on Earth through her different aspects and facets. *I am the heart energy of the Divine Mother as are Kwan Yin , Aphrodite, and Venus, among others.* When you invoke the Hathor symbol, which are the solar and lunar discs in the boat of Ra, you open your heart within free will to high frequencies of trust. Love and prosperity become natural outcomes of this loving flowing state of being.

When you invoke me through the symbology of the mirror of Hathor, you connect to the energy of the mirroring aspects of your reality where the Universal Law of "as within so without" triggers and exists.

Bast

When you invoke Goddess Bast, you connect to the energy of divine play and joy. Bast is the Cat Goddess that connects you to the lightness of your being. This Divine play of the creator is known as Lila in Sanskrit. Neter Bast is great for the invocation of good fortune, music, dance, and joy. She can also help you heal spiritually.

Osiris

Osiris connects you to the archetypal energy of the tree of life and the Divine Father energies. By invoking the Neter Osiris you make a strong connection to the energy of devotion, wisdom, spiritual strength, and also to the energies of justice, integrity, and responsibility. You can use this powerful archetypal energy in a sacred way to invoke greater security , stability, growth, and fertility.

Horus

The Neter Horus connects you to the energy of the all-pervading, all-knowing inner eye which is called the third eye; and to its place between your eyebrows. This energy is particularly powerful for healing, courage, harmony, creativity, beauty, and the home.

Neter Horus was very much at one with the spiritual energy, love, and power of his father Osiris. This gave the total power and hundred percent opening of his third eye, his intuitive link with source. Therefore when you connect to this divine archetypal energy, it can begin to connect you and open up your connection to the Divine Father energies of the universe. Your psychic and intuitive abilities can begin to blossom and grow through meditation on Neter.

Ptah

Neter Ptah is the archetypal energy of the divine architect of the universe and a great Being of Light and unconditional love. On the spiritual realm he can help you with the building of the Temple of the Spiritual Identity. In the mental and subconscious realms he can help connect you to your animus, your male energies, and to the energy of responsibility, invention, skill, and ingenuity.

· PTAH

In the mental and subconscious realms he can help connect you to your animus, your male energies, and to the energy of responsibility, invention, skill, and ingenuity.

Thoth

Lord Thoth is the scribe of the universe and gave your world the written script. He can also be invoked to connect to the archetypal energy of healing for powerful and sometimes immediate results.

All the archetypal energies are great tools for coming into deep states of meditation, especially the energy of Lord Thoth. He is also the Lord of Time, the God of Magic and Medicine, Scribe to the Gods, Patron of Healers and Keeper of the Akashic Records. Invoke and meditate upon his energy for the healing of Karma to come into nonjudgment, for health issues and charismatic communication and writing. All issues around education also come within his jurisdiction.

Anubis

Neter Anubis, as I have mentioned before, is the keeper of the galactic night and protects you through the healing of your shadow self and the dark night of the soul on its journey to the Light. He is the guardian against the forces of the lower astral planes. He is granted special rites to free and safe access through all undesirable regions or realms. *He can protect you at all levels and obstacles on the spiritual path.* You can also invoke him for strengthening of the qualities of diplomacy, humor, and fearlessness.

Some Sacred Archetypal Symbols

Lotus

Let me tell you of the magic of the archetypal energy of the Lotus. *This is the sacred flower of ancient Egypt.* The lotus is a vehicle for astral travel for the Goddess. It connects to all the sacred elements: earth through its roots, water as it grows in water, and air as it floats on water connecting to the atmosphere. It receives the light of the sun and its fire to grow and bloom; and when you meditate on the energy of the lotus, as do many Buddhists through the invocation of Lord Buddha's famous Lotus Sutra, you connect to the sacred element of ether. By invoking this powerful energy during meditation, you go into deep states of your being and into a transcendence of the mind. Lotus is also useful for invoking peace and harmony.

Scarab

The Scarab in ancient Egypt was symbolic for shedding of the old to make way for the new and higher state of consciousness.

Scarab can be invoked to aid in letting go of relationships; material possessions; and also thoughts, memories, and attitudes that no longer serve your higher good— to allow creating a space to bring in the new. Through this Divine Archetypal energy you can begin to shift from lamenting your losses to the joy of renewal. The Scarab represents rebirth, creation, and restoration of life. This energy is fabulously useful in this time of change to help you to skip gracefully through change to grand new beginnings. Invoke scarab to come to a deep sense of acceptance on all issues that require a shift of attitude.

> ## SCARAB
>
> Through this Divine Archetypal energy you can begin to shift from lamenting your losses to the joy of renewal.

Pyramid

The pyramid represents manifestation and a coming out of the four directions to an ascending state of being and becoming. The pyramid is also an instrument that may be used to step down higher frequencies from ascended dimensions for accelerated transformation and healing of third-dimensional consciousness. The great pyramid of Giza was used and is being reactivated in current time to step down the fifth-dimensional energies and healing from Sirius. The Mayans used, and still do use, their pyramids for similar purpose.

One of the most powerful tools used by fifth-dimensional beings to raise consciousness and step up frequency is through the use of sacred geometry. There is evidence all over your planet in various periods of your history of these divine symbols in art, especially in Egypt. In current time, a lot of this sacred divine knowledge and symbols has been given back to you at an accelerated rate through various levels of Reiki initiations. What would have taken many years or lifetimes to achieve in the initiatory process of esoteric wisdom, is being given to you in weekend courses and with shorter and shorter periods for assimilation to the next step of the attunement ladder. *As many of you know, Reiki means universal life-force energy.* Egyptian Reiki is currently being taught to you as the systems of mastery within Sekhem, Seichim, Seichem, Karuna® Reiki, and the Egyptian Cartouche. There are variations to some of these systems. *As I have mentioned before, the time of secrets is coming to an end, as some of your authors have illustrated through disclosure of the sacred symbols in their books.*

Sacred geometry is used in many other streams of spiritual understanding. Ancient Egypt was greatly influenced by this esoteric understanding of divine symbology. Sacred geometry is a tool for you as humanity to use to wake up to higher, expanded awareness as we come out of the third and into the fifth dimension beyond linear time and space. This is why Reiki has spread all over the planet in the last twenty years and been used as a wondrous tool by the spiritual hierarchy to raise consciousness. Sacred geometry is an easy and quick way to assist in creating sacred and nurturing spaces for the healing and the opening of your human heart. As you do this and become well versed in wise open heartedness, you will begin to open up and link in to your multi-dimensional heart-felt states of being and becoming.

The archetypal energy of the Sacred Pyramid connects you deeply to your intrinsic, eternal timeless nature and helps you go beyond old limitations to expanded consciousness. It can also be invoked to assist in the qualities of reliability and balanced conservation.

Sirius

Invoking the energy of Sirius strongly connects you to the energy of Universal awareness, pioneering spirit, adventure, the frequencies of the Age of Aquarius, and the deprogramming of limiting concepts. This archetypal energy is powerful for inculcating open-mindfulness.

Crook and Flail

The symbols of the Crook and Flail were invoked in my temples by my initiates to strengthen the energies of balanced authority, discipline to help with the mastery of the ego, and to increase self-confidence. The divine authority of the Pharaohs of ancient Egypt was symbolized and represented by their carrying of the crook and flail across their Divine hearts. The Crook represented the intuitive or lunar aspect and the Flail the solar or authorities aspect.

> The symbols of the Crook and Flail . . .
> strengthen the energies of balanced authority,
> and foster discipline to help with the mastery of
> the ego and to increase self-confidence.

Sacred Serpent

The sacred serpent of ancient Egypt or Uraeus may be invoked to amplify your wisdom energies. *It is a powerful symbol of your Kundalini energy as it rises up your spine to higher states of wisdom and enlightenment.* All Goddesses of ancient Egypt wore wondrous Uraeus cobras wrapped around their heads with the cobra's hood protecting and opening their third eyes. This represents the wisdom energy of the Goddess. In ancient Egypt in my Mystery Schools snake initiations were also conducted to help initiates overcome fear. Connecting to Uraeus during meditation can help you to increase your spiritual integrity and sagacity.

Great Sphinx of Giza

The Great Sphinx of Gizeh is a wondrous symbol of the unification of our animalistic nature with our Divine Spirit. It also shows you clearly that there are many other forms of consciousness and being in the universe. When you invoke this powerful deep archetypal symbol, you connect strongly to the energy of patience, to the energy of detached witnessing, and to the energy of nonjudgmental observation. Patience on the path was a most essential requirement for spiritual initiates at all levels in the Mystery Schools of Hathor.

Patience is the calm acceptance of Divine timing and of the eternal nature of all things beyond time. The tendency of the mind is to push you into impatience, which then leads to frustration and disease. The intrinsic nature of your human heart in its depth of Divine connection is patient, ever patient. The Sphinx is a grand reminder of this eternal nature of Divinity that can exist happily in time and beyond time.

> Patience is the calm acceptance of Divine timing and of the eternal nature of all things beyond time.

Ankh

The Ankh is the symbol of the key to immortal life. The Gods and Goddesses are often portrayed with the Ankh held before their mouth representing the gift of immortal life and wondrous life-force energy. Invocation of the Ankh energies connects you to your immortal nature of Universal Love and to balanced existence. This integration and connection to the female within and without can help greatly in the business of romance. The Ankh represents deep harmony.

10

TIME TO WAKE UP

SOME OF YOUR PLEIADIAN and Sirian brothers and sisters from higher consciousness are strongly working towards the divine plan for six billion plus humans to wake up to Christ consciousness (which I have said is unity consciousness) between now, 2012, and beyond. This sort of experiment has never been performed in the universe and therefore even the creator is not certain of the outcome. This is because he/she has given you free will which gives you the full opportunity to choose total destruction instead (as you did at the end of the Atlantean period).

The Divine Mother cajoles, inspires, and tickles you to choosing "heaven on Earth" as opposed to apocalyptic scenarios. The poles are shifting, the ice caps are currently melting and Earth is moving from the third to the fifth dimension. So it is quite a practical choice to go with the flow of the river of change rather than against it. *If you use even one of my keys with sincerity of intention it will open the magnificent door to your incredible human heart, which will become a portal of transcendence and strengthening of the Christ* grid. As you become unconditionally loving. whole, and complete, you will help others through your frequency to open their hearts. When you reach the critical mass of fully awakened human beings, then you will take all six billion with you to the higher harmonic of agape-Christ consciousness. Therein will begin the incredible journey of Earth and her peoples into higher dimensions.

Many of you as teachers and healers of the spiritual path seem to think you can achieve higher states of esoteric awareness while somehow bypassing the healing of your central sun within you, your heart. This is a faulty understanding. I observe that many of you have your crown chakra and third eye open and connected to very high vibrational states and yet the heart remains broken, hurt, or only conditionally opened. As I keep repeating, it is of utmost importance to have a balanced opening and clearing of all your chakras in order for you not to slip backwards on the ascension spiral. *Any kind of spiritual teaching or healing that ultimately bypasses the temple of the human heart, cannot achieve the goal of the human being reawakening to the divinity within themselves and the reflection of this inner goddess self in all that is.* Use your intuition and intent to attract heartfelt teachers and healers and you will step into accelerated DNA activation and awakening.

As I have said, healing occurs in layers and yet a balance is required not to go over the same dramas too many times as some of you love to do in spiritual workshop after workshop. The more efficiently you heal your unresolved aspects of self the greater will be your ability to help others and Mother Earth heal to divert drastic Earth changes and instead bring heaven to Earth.

The Goddess is awakening in all human hearts everywhere. Slumber time is over. But there is no waking up for a closed, numb heart.

Nurturing the temple of your heart is of utmost importance in these times of accelerated change and transformation. Transcendental love beckons you to a universe of magic and mystery. It is time for human beings to rebirth themselves into the Gods and Goddesses that they always were but may have forgotten. Let me, Goddess Hathor, inspire you, and lift you out of the mire into the realm of exalted living, being, and creating. What could be more exciting and/or inspiring?

The living light energy of Sekhem is here to help you move forwards in love and trust. As you heal and also strengthen your simple spiritual practices, you move into Unity Consciousness more deeply. In this state, loving others comes naturally, as they are seen experientially as aspects of the same Divine Self.

> In this state, loving others comes naturally,
> as they are seen experientially as aspects
> of the same Divine Self.

Meditation on the Infinity symbol in the Heart is a dynamic way to connect to the oneness in all living Beings and nonliving matter. Altruism is the name of the current Divine game. Here the practice of Divine Balance is imperative . *You cannot help others from a state of depletion.* So giving and nurturing has to begin with the self, i.e., yourself. Once you start becoming more meditative, silent, and begin your own healing, you can take baby steps towards the nurturing and healing of others. Whenever helping yourself and others heal, remember to align your intended healing energy with God/Goddess.

Walking Your Talk

I would like to talk to you about walking your talk. You don't have to be perfectly healed and enlightened before you start sharing and participating in the healing journey of animals, mother nature, and your fellow sisters and brothers. However, to put all your energy and focus on the healing and "fixing" of others will not work. Remember that you only act as a mirror for another being's healing. Basically the other heals himself. The clearer, more centered and integrated you are yourself on the issue to be healed, the more powerful will be your healing mirror of Hathor for the other. Just talking about high-faluting spiritual concepts and ideals is not going to work as you step more and more into the fifth-dimensional frequencies of light and love.

In the fifth-dimension which is beyond time and space, your emotions and thoughts and intentions manifest instantaneously. Therefore you need to be very clear and have pure heartfelt channels before you move more strongly into fifth-dimensional orientation. Impeccability of intent and a high degree of integrity is now being asked of you as you step into your Goddess nature. What does this mean? *It means to begin to practice more and more strongly with each day matching your thoughts and words with your actions.* As an emanation of the cosmic Christ, Sai Baba says, "the hands that work are greater than the hands that pray." This is a time to become a spiritual warrior in action!

Ritual and ceremony, prayer and meditation are all very useful and important in this wake-up cycle. However, acting your truth, speaking it and living it is what the current game is all about. As I have said before, the manifestations are becoming more and more instantaneous. Therefore it is spiritual intelligence to begin to clean up your thoughts and actions in order not to keep slipping back into the pain and dramas, the conflict of duality.

Judgment

One of the most important things to drop in this current time is judgment; judgment of yourself and judgment of others. It is time to release your guilt and the morphogenic regrets of your ancestors. If you find yourself judging, practice laughing at your mind chatter, forgive yourself, embrace the negative thoughts and feelings and then let them go. As I have said before, if you are patient and wait long enough, all your negative thoughts, and particularly emotions such as anger and jealousy, will come back to the polarity, which is love. This is called converting your poisons into honey. I, or any other aspect of the Goddess, am here to help you transmute negativity and prejudice. As Jesus said, "Ask and you shall receive." You must remember to ask, for you operate within the law of free will, and the Divine will assist you on request.

Silence

Silence and time alone are great qualities to assist you into a manifest space of peace and serenity. It is very difficult for you to do this until you switch off your mobile phones, computers, TVs, and so on. It is a good idea to get out of the habit of always using your car and to learn to walk or cycle instead. I observe that many of you are choosing to jump out of airplanes or jump into cars or onto roller coasters—anything to get away from spending intimate time with yourselves. Nothing wrong with these vehicles of movement, they are fine. However spending time with oneself without these distractions is important. Using wisdom and intuition to decide when to create pollution (i.e., through the use of these vehicles) and when to refrain will bring you into greater sensitivity and Grace.

Unless you learn to be okay with being by yourself and simply being, you can never learn to love others, because you don't even know in this case who you are and how you feel. Things are speeding up and will continue to speed up at a faster pace, and therefore *the key to balance* is finding quality time on a regular basis to slow down and be still. The heart begins to open more readily in peaceful, silent, still spaces. *Once you become good at instilling the state of beingness, you will be able to invoke it even in loud and chaotic scenarios.* During the time spent in silence and stillness you connect strongly to the realm of the unmanifest Divine Source within yourself. As Jesus the great teacher of the heart says, "Be still and know."

Once you learn to make a strong connection and build an intimate relationship with the silent unmanifest realm, you can begin to manifest consciously. You can become the consciously co-creating God/Goddess that you are. You begin to remember and your ancient eyes of inner knowingness begin to open. Your Heart feels safe and centered. You open your heart in wise and protected spaces informed by intuition and your sense of knowingness.

What Makes Your Heart Sing?

The Goddess is here to beckon you into these wonderful new vistas of being and becoming. So I would like to ask you: *what makes your heart sing?* I can see many of you thinking "I don't know," or "It's really hard for me to feel how I feel." When asked how you feel or to feel something, it is a human tendency of many of you to immediately think how you feel. This is missing the boat to the river of your heart.

You can begin by breathing into your heart, sitting in quiet meditation and imagining sinking your mind into the blue light of your heart. The more powerfully you know and trust that your intention will manifest, the more strongly you will achieve this state of no mind. It requires practice. As you begin to feel comfortable focusing on the energy and love of your heart, it will slowly but surely start speaking to you in soft subtle whispers. Or instead, you may have a flash of deep knowingness.

I observe many of you have not yet realized the difference between thinking how you feel about something and actually knowing how you feel. As I have said many times before, one of the most important subjects of the Heart Mystery school of Hathor was and is, *feeling your feelings, dealing with feeling,* and *healing through feeling.* My initiates in ancient Egypt learned and experienced the deep connection between the emotional body and the spiritual body or Ba, (the/your) immortal soul. There is no question of progressing spiritually without the clearing and healing of your feeling body, your emotions. As you do this, you come to be in the present moment and the power of the Now. You become more spontaneously joyful, and co-creative as opposed to only reactive. As you combine the healing of your emotions with meditation, you come into the integration of the mind and the heart, and your heart begins to blossom into compassion, passion, and song.

> There is no question of progressing spiritually without the clearing and healing of your feeling body, your emotions.

By stepping deeper and deeper into this state, you begin to become as clear as a bell and then this bell can sing the melody of your heart moment-to-moment. Very easily, you can begin to move into blissful and ecstatic states of consciousness. *If you ask a little child what makes their heart sing, they are spontaneous, instantaneous, and passionate; they know the answer. So learn from your children and become child-like.*

Most of you, I observe, have begun to realize that blindly wanting the things and the types of relationships marketed by your media or sought after by your peers and conditioning is not making you peaceful, joyful, and happy-hearted. So a joyful heart is about the courage to, as I have said, be still and find out what your heart desires and what makes your heart sing.

Simplicity

Simplicity is the golden key to an intimate and loving relationship with your beauteous heart. There is no delicious spiritual pie without generous dashes of simplicity. Babaji, also known as Bhole Baba, exemplifies the Simplicity Principle magnificently. Bhole means simple. He happens to be a most wondrous, heartfelt avatar (direct emanation of source). Jesus too was simple and Buddha gained enlightenment through giving up internal and external complexity. I would like you to note that being simple does not mean you have to be poor. If you have less, you can enjoy the freedom it brings: if you have great flow, you can enjoy a different kind of freedom. It is totally possible to be abundant and yet simple. The vital issue is to be detached from your possessions and relationships and yet enjoy them, but be willing to let go based on the intuition and the wisdom of the Now.

> There is no delicious spiritual pie without generous dashes of simplicity.

In the Golden Ages of Ancient Egypt, the most beautiful and awe-inspiring cultures flourished and bloomed. There was a great emphasis on internal and external intuitive Feng Shui. The focus for initiates of the Mystery Schools was inner and outer beauty and aesthetic balance. It was all about heaven on Earth and a bringing down of super-conscious energy amongst men and women of the time. In spite of great opulence and abundant flow, the paradox of

Simplicity was still very much honored and practiced. Any initiate at any level who got too attached to anything (including the high priests/priestesses, the esoteric wisdom, or grand ritual and ceremony) fell from grace.

In this time (2010), and as you dance towards the end of time, 2012 and beyond, materialism and complexity—mental, spiritual, and material have reached the ultimate pinnacle of excess as opposed to success. If what you own is like a huge burden on your back, (whether material possessions, over-intellectualized thoughts, or chaotic and complicated emotional relationships), how can you call this being successful? For many of you, I observe this seems to be how you think and feel about success. Many of you blindly ape the icons of your time—superstars, pop stars, and the like, even when in some cases you clearly see that they are not necessarily happy or peaceful in spite of great fame and wealth. As I have said before, to be wealthy or even famous in and of itself is not a bad thing. It is all about detachment, and most importantly, about balance. Money and wealth are ultimately energy. Therefore, in order to enjoy large amounts of money, you need to balance and match your acquisitions with your wisdom if you want to be an integrated spiritual initiate.

When you achieve greater levels of openheartedness in your relationship with yourself or significant others (or to humanity as a whole), you also automatically and gracefully open yourself up to receive the abundant flow of the universe. This includes the plentiful supply of energy, time, money, fun, and love.

I feel the pain of many of you as you seem to struggle with the issue of lack. Many of you, including those of you who pride yourself for having been on strong spiritual paths over many years, still find yourself lacking in time, money, energy, and love. It is important to note that any form of lack reflects negative thinking and negative emotions around being innocent, being guilt-free, and being deserving. *The truth is that there is plenty of time and you are eternal and also that time can be bent.* The past, present, and future from a higher perspective occur simultaneously like several tracks of music all playing at the same time. So it is time now to make time your servant and to let go of being its slave. This is easily done by coming into the present eternal moment of Now and through meditation. If you intend time to bend, you can begin to achieve this more and more with ever-stronger results, through practice.

> The truth is that there is plenty of time and you are eternal and also that time can be bent.

11

QUALITIES OF OPENHEARTED BEINGNESS

I OBSERVE THAT MANY humans are using their business as a way to avoid an intimate relationship with their hearts and to somehow bypass having loving relationships with others. The mind plays a big role in this roller coaster game of keeping you in complexity, in a whirlwind of activity and mental jabber. So it is your choice to come out of feeling like a victim of your societies, systems, and businesses. It would behoove you to choose the business of stillness and simplicity as opposed to the business of busyness. A simple person is one who engages in that which her intuition guides her moment to moment. *A simple person is very happy just being, trusting, and relaxing.* He/she knows that the Divine Cosmic Energy is moving worlds and planets and she can let go and relax into graceful effortless manifestation of her heart's desires.

> So it is your choice to come out of feeling like a victim of your societies, systems, and businesses.

> It would behoove you to choose the business
> of stillness and simplicity as opposed to the
> business of busyness.

For each of you now it is imperative to begin drastic internal and external Feng Shui and space clearing: both the inner space and the outer space! What I notice is that some of you have achieved high states of inner peace and spiritual understanding and yet choose to live in squalor or unaesthetic surroundings. It is important for the inner to reflect the outer and the outer to reflect the inner state of your being. Only then do you come into the spiritual alignment of integrity and love. The heart is all-inclusive, all embracing as part of its intrinsic nature. So balancing all aspects of your reality to align with walking your talk is important.

> Love does not exclude anything, whereas the
> mind is exclusive in its orientation.

Responsibility

You are not a victim. You are a powerful spiritual entity having a human experience on earth—here, now. Therefore by changing your negative thoughts, expectations, and emotional states to positive programming, and by coming into a state of knowingness and trust, you easily move out of victimhood and struggle. This allows you to move into creating heaven on Earth and creating great flow not only for yourself but all who touch your path. If you think you can, you can! Many of the current New Age books on your planet are teaching you currently about cosmic ordering and manifesting.

When your heart is tightly closed and your mind is rambling on, you immediately stop true flow. When you open the heart, you create space to receive: and by intending that the very best in life come to you easily, joyfully, and harmoniously; that is what you create on the canvass of your life.

> When you open the heart, you create space to receive: and by intending that the very best in life come to you easily, joyfully, and harmoniously; that is what you create on the canvass of your life.

The Keys of Hathor (such as breathing, meditating, chanting, healing through sacred sound, and mantra repetition), together with celebration and initiation to higher energy, all help to begin the process of trusting and relaxing. Greater trust and relaxation allows the flow of Universal wealth and energy to come in and through you for the blessing of man/womankind.

As the cosmic energies of source intensify in the run up to 2012 and beyond, do you find yourself more and more exhausted and lacking in energy? Remember, you have made many collective agreements within the holographic nature of your reality. One of them is to go through disease, old age, and for a lot of you, death by the age of seventy or eighty. You can come out of this paradigm and choose through intention and focus to live as long as you like and in a state of youthfulness and abundant energy. It is up to you.

Some of you, it is wondrous to see, have a deep knowing of being a body of light, becoming lighter and lighter and grounding this light on planet Earth. You know that instead of choosing to die in your human body, in the time to come you will choose to ascend as a ball of light into the unified field of light. Many of you in the world of New Age consciousness are familiar with the concept of *ascension* and *immortality*. It is a grave mistake to believe that ascension is about spacing out, getting ungrounded, going up into your head, into the super intellectualization of spiritual wisdom, and/or dropping or copping out. As I keep repeating, this is a time of stepping down the high vibrational energy of heaven fifth-dimension and beyond, marrying it into the temples of your third-dimension bodies and grounding it on Earth.

Gaia is rebirthing herself into the marriage of matter and spirit as we speak. This is a phenomenon beyond the direct comprehension of the mind. It can be best understood in states of spiritual trance and meditation as well as during states of Unity Consciousness and initiation into ascended frequency.

Your scientists, especially physicists, are beginning to slowly catch up with metaphysics. They now know that you are not as solid and dense as you think you are, nor is matter (as solid and dense as previously thought), i.e., stones and planets. They know scientifically that when you go to the subatomic levels you are 99.9 percent hyperspace.

The quantum physicists currently also know that a particle can exist simultaneously in two places at the same time. This proves what metaphysics has always known, which is the nature of your multidimensional being. This is a good time to step gracefully out of linear thinking and being into expansive, unlimited, cosmic, harmonious states of Being.

Ultimately you are an expanded body of light and sound. *Without getting too complicated about this,* as you heal all residual unresolved issues of thoughts, words, emotions, and pain of lifetimes, you become lighter and lighter and more present to the power of the Now moment.

Basically, heaven is already within you. As you clean the electromagnetic mirror of your soul, and past and present karma is dissolved, you become simple: *you become the detached witness of All that Is.* You see yourself in the manifest and the unmanifest reality everywhere and nowhere.

> As you clean the electromagnetic mirror of your soul, and past and present karma is dissolved, you become simple: you become the detached witness of All that Is.

As you embody the full experience of your body of light, you will increase the gifts of clairaudience, telepathy, teleportation, clairsentience, and so on. This occurs because you move out of the consciousness of yourself as a separate solid entity into the field of nonduality and then into the unified field from which all things come and in which all things are possible.

Courage

I wish, as a heartfelt aspect of the Divine Mother energy, to speak to you of *courage* on your journey back to a blossoming whole and complete healthy heart. Many of you are well acquainted with the energy of being spiritual warriors on the path to higher consciousness. *There is no question of being safe to open your heart to greater unconditional love without inculcating a deep reconnection to the courage of your soul.* This is because openheartedness demands you to follow your own inner authority as opposed to the demands and commands of authority and conditioning outside of yourself. Being unconditionally loving is not about pleasing others, it is not even about essentially "fitting in," and it is certainly not about having the most comfortable or quiet life in the short and medium term.

> There is no question of being safe to open your heart to greater unconditional love without inculcating a deep reconnection to the courage of your soul.
>
> Openheartedness demands you to follow your own inner authority as opposed to the demands and commands of authority and conditioning outside of yourself.

If you are flowering in a state of open-hearted courageous living, many will feel threatened, upset, or even attacked in some cases by your energy. This is because in a state of courageous heartfelt being, your energy field becomes a mirror and brings up all that is less than all-love for examination. So those who are in extreme states of separation and mind control will even want to avoid you altogether. Open heartedness is passionate, and an intense state of being and becoming. As Bhole Baba says "Think your own thoughts and be your own person." He also says "Do not lean on the borrowed staff of another." What this means is, by all means share, give and receive, love and support, but remember to balance it with becoming whole and complete *within yourself* and not dependent and needy in the long term. *Practicing these teachings will connect you powerfully to inner self-love, detachment, and intuitive wisdom of when to open up and when to veil the light of your love.* Love uses intuitive wisdom moment-to-moment spontaneously and based on what feels right as each bridge of experiential drama is crossed.

> Practicing these teachings will connect you powerfully to inner self-love, detachment, and intuitive wisdom of when to open up and when to veil the light of your love.

Being a spiritual warrior is not about being defiant just for the sake of being defiant, but it is about being courageous and brave— even to stand against the whole world if you believe in something truly and deeply and have a strong sense of knowing. It has to feel very right in your being and ultimately you have to cross-check whether it is in synergy with the Highest Good of All Concerned. For example, the entity Christopher Columbus had the courage to be a pioneer and burst the paradigm of a flat world, to be replaced by the more correct hypothesis that your planet is actually round. This is very important, as the mind will oftentimes pretend to be your heart energy or the energy of your intuitive wisdom.

> The mind will oftentimes pretend to be your heart energy or the energy of your intuitive wisdom.

In each decision, just ask yourself what would love choose?—not narrow separate love, but unconditional love that is all-inclusive. It is important to note that until your reach a state of total enlightenment and heart centeredness, to be careful and more conscious of the energies you wish to interact with and the energies you don't. It is also not about forcing others to choose the spiritual path but giving them the space if they so choose to learn the lessons of darkness of separation and of not feeling and healing.

A spiritual warrior is very balanced between the polarities and the extremes. To go to an extreme polarity from time to time can be ok as long as you have one part of your consciousness centered. Concentration or focus on your pranic tube (the central energy column that connects all chakras in a straight line) is a practical means of maintaining centeredness, and a connection to heaven and Earth.

One of the biggest hurdles to the safe opening of your hearts is the obvious fear of opening and being vulnerable. This is where the quality of courage greatly facilitates strengthening the quality of vulnerability and openness that are all essential ingredients for baking an openhearted delicious cake of unconditional love. So the question comes up, when to take a risk and when to stay protected and closed? The more regularly you meditate and spend time alone, the more connected you become to your intuition and self-love; and then the more you trust your love of self, the more easily this love is able to spill out and embrace other aspects of self as guided by a centered and wise heart. By taking little risks as opposed to blindly opening up to the love frequencies that do not serve your Higher Good, you softly, softly go through an alchemy that makes it safer and more balanced to open up further. When there is deep love, deep fear will come up. When it does, as the great Pleiadian being Ptah says,

1. Take off your head, i.e., ignore thinking.

2. Embrace the feeling, i.e., *embrace the fear* as you would a hurt child to your bosom and then,

3. You are ready to go through the fear and choose love.

I would like you to understand that all things are interconnected and part of a harmonious whole, including that which seems to be "inharmonious." So as you practice strengthening and anchoring yourself into any one of the qualities required for true openheartedness, you simultaneously create an opening and strengthen all the other qualities. For example, if you face your fear and risk loving in a balanced intuitive gentle way, you strengthen the quality of intelligent vulnerability (which is a strength not a weakness) automatically.

Acceptance is essential to any spiritual aspirant: the wise acceptance of whatever is occurring, no matter how one judges it, moment-to-moment. This is something that the initiate practices quietly at the core of his being. It does not mean that you do not practice discernment and it also does not mean you are not allowed to say "no." I notice that most human beings feel and think that loving whole-heartedly involves pleasing the other totally and saying yes to everything. This is a major mistake of understanding.

Most of you know about tough love and how often saying "no," walking away, or actually putting up a centered open-hearted fight may be essential. The entity Mahatma Gandhi illustrates fighting the "good fight" without resorting to violence and being oppositional, by his use of peaceful noncooperation. You may choose to have a differing view from your fellow human beings in some cases, yet still it is important to honor the views of others and give them the space to learn their lessons if they choose not to see a higher more heartfelt perspective—even though you have offered it. In other words, the total acceptance of the nonacceptance of others as part of their free will is wise understanding.

If you can balance opposing that which you are guided by your heart and soul energy to oppose with honoring your opponent and their perspective at the same time, you have truly mastered unconditional love and spiritual warriorship. The important thing in all cases of inner and outer conflict is to stay connected to your spiritual anchor point; and dance with the consciousness of all things—the awareness that all beings are ultimately part of the same Unified Field of Energy and Awareness.

Also you will find to your surprised delight that the more deeply and sincerely you practice acceptance and embracement of your internal and external dramas, the less you will need to engage in deep and intense conflict and opposition. In many cases the peaceful, loving vibrations of your energy field will rub off onto others and help bring them to peace without force.

Giving and Sharing

As the wondrous human being Dr. Deepak Chopra most eloquently explains in his book on Vedantic Wisdom, the *Seven Spiritual Laws of Success*—giving (sharing) is one of the priceless jewels in the Crown of Open-heartedness. I note with dismay that many of you in the New Age movement seem to have gotten into an imbalance of groundedness and the manifestation of plenty, while using "being on a spiritual path" as the excuse. *Being spiritual does not mean a state of lack.* This was most beautifully illustrated in the Golden Ages that I, Goddess Hathor, showed in Ancient Egypt before the corruption and decline. As Jesus said, "the Kingdom of Heaven is within you." He did not say "the world of lack is within you." To just chase riches without it being balanced with integrity and deep spiritual wisdom causes suffering and a lack of joy. The magic of creating plentiful flow of time, energy, love, and money, comes through the continuous practice of sharing and giving.

Some of you are happy to be most generously giving to your self but are totally blocked in giving to others. Others amongst you, I note, create a total imbalance by over-giving and unwise giving to others while giving nothing to yourself. Wherever you are stuck, if you just start by checking in and beginning to give to yourself and others whatever it is you lack in a balanced way, you trigger the law of manifestation and law of attraction of similar frequency. In all spiritual practice, balance is the key. The sacred symbol of infinity is the key, "as within, so without," "as above, so below"—microcosm, macrocosm. *In the Divine Infinity symbol, both loops representing the inner and outer are equal. One is not larger than the other. Remember this.*

As you now know, there is only one Unified Field of Consciousness that manifests as plants, stones, planets, and individual human beings, etc. *So in this time of a quantum leap of consciousness, just giving and just loving yourself, your family, your country will not work.* You are being impulsed and inspired to open your heart to all of humanity as part of the global family, and to the animals and Mother Nature in the same way. So giving through intuitive intelligence, wisely, with generosity, moment-to-moment—to oneself and others—opens you up to deeper compassion, richness of love, joy, and plenty. Also here, the law of circulation comes into play. *The more you keep energy moving the more it amplifies.* Money is energy. This does not mean creating the imbalance of extreme indebtedness and/or using your giving to manipulate, control, and "please others." Balance, Balance, Balance.

Peace and Silence

When you invoke the archetypal energy of Hathor you can, through intention, quickly access your inner temple of peace and silence. Without creating regular sacred space for peace and silence, there is no question of the heart wanting to open in safety, joy, and inspiration. When you have the tendency to force open your heart through the aggressive use of your mind (and through traumatic and violent feelings, emotions, or reactive conditioning of this or past lives), your heart may at times open, but it will be traumatic and painful. The more you practice this kind of dysfunctional behavior the less willing your heart becomes to trust you and trust the process of safe, sacred, loving, wise opening.

So bypassing peace on the path to your heart is not the preferred choice for achieving a safe heartfelt state. When you spend time alone doing nothing but trusting and relaxing, time in nature communing with the elements, and time just "being" to enjoy and to be silent, you come into an easy state of bliss and ecstasy. This favorable result is not achieved immediately. *In the beginning you may feel uncomfortable about an intimate journey with yourself and the whisperings of your heart.* You may find your mind kicking and screaming and you may also feel extremely uncomfortable about not "doing" and "having a break from incessant busyness." This is where chanting, meditation, invoking of higher beings such as Buddha or Kwan Yin or myself can be extremely effective to help begin the powerful journey of becoming the detached witness of your thoughts, emotions, and body. Music, dance, intelligent fasting, and unplugging your gizmos are joyful ways to step into the realm of the unmanifest, the silence, the peace that is deep within your inner temple of the self.

As you become better and better at creating peace within yourself, remember to release negative thoughts and emotions by (1) watching them, (2) dis-identifying from them, and (3) choosing to come back each time to the castle of Nepthys or magical void within you. The deeper into your peace you go (even if it feels very scary in the beginning), the more creative, dynamic, and inspired you become in your time allocated to "doing." *You begin to find, to your delight, that everything you need to achieve or become or create occurs effortlessly and easily in a field of trusting and relaxing.* This is choosing through the Divine qualities of peace, creative and harmonious living and Being, as opposed to destructive, unbalanced, reactive states of being and doing.

Most of you want peace on Earth, peace among nations, and peace between men and women and within families. Your tendency is often to try and fix the problem of a lack of peace on the outside or to go into blame of your parents, teachers, governments, and other authority figures. This is a grave mistake that leads to war and further disruption and chaos. The key to peace (as the amazing being of light, St. Germain, exemplifies), is to become acquainted with your inner world; your inner prejudices, judgments, and feelings of lack and aggression. Anger very often has its root in suppressed or denied pain and/or deep chronic frustration. Frustration often builds up within you to a diabolic proportion as a result of persistent indulgence in the feeling of victimhood and helplessness. Remember, "As you sow, so shall you reap."

Remember, your thoughts and feelings about things create your reality 100 per cent. So if you want peace, become peace. If you wish for joy and bliss, convert your poisons into honey and become a larger and larger force field of bubbling and effervescent ecstasy. *All this information is going to make some of you very cross.* Some of you are thinking it is not so simple. "It is not so easy." "I can't do it." Or, "How dare the Goddess take away my comfy teddy bear of blame and shame and my comfy slippers of suffering and lack?" *I am not taking away anything.* I am just here with a lot of love and compassion for the broken heartedness of humanity and a lot of compassion for the denied and suppressed broken heartedness of a vast number of you on Earth now. I am here, as I keep reiterating, to cajole you, tickle you, and inspire you into choosing to awaken to your God/Goddess nature and into a more expanded realm of possibilities and choices that are divinely guided for bringing heaven to Earth and heaven into your lives and hearts. This does of course require the letting go of that which you perceive as hell in your life and on Earth.

It really is so simple. But it does require, paradoxically, daily practice and awareness. As you become an anchored, grounded force field of unified peace and harmony, you will become more and more well-versed in maintaining and holding the energy of peace within you. This peace within you and your field or aura, will be beneficial for yourself and others, even in chaotic, loud, disruptive environments. You have seen your saints and other enlightened beings like Mother Theresa do this time and time again.

Remember what you focus on is what you get. If you focus on war you will get more war. *If you focus on peace and become peace you will inspire many others to choose the same frequency, and war will become a thing of the past.* This is the Divine Plan for Earth in the coming times. *Om Shanti, Shanti, Shanti* (Peace within, Peace without, Peace to all beings everywhere). Ultimately, if you are brave enough to clear the weeds of doubt, fear, pain, trauma, and other unwanted emotional paraphernalia, you come to a pristine garden of inner peace that is your birthright and a natural state of being. Letting go of the comfy habit of staying at war with yourself; of judgment and conflict with self and others has to be weeded out. What are you going to choose? To let your mind with its tendency to doubt, fear, and separate be the captain of your ship, or to choose consciously to allow and reinstate the supremacy of your soul energy (your Higher Self) to be commander as you sail effortlessly over an ocean of living light, harmony, and balance?

Harmony and Beauty

The heart thrives and flourishes in the energy of harmony and beauty. It finds beauty in even the simplest things. What do you understand of the harmonic of harmony? In music, as you know, you can create celestial melodies or you can choose to create cacophony and noise. By starting simply and reducing unnecessary complexity and inner and outer clutter, you begin to create magnificently beautiful and harmonious surroundings, interiors, and atmospheres for yourself and others. Your mind and your conditioning often teach you to hoard and accumulate the unnecessary. *Letting go of that which no longer serves you—be it people, places, things, ideas, or emotions—is all part of the fantastic journey back to simply beautiful and harmonious living and being.*

In your current history, it has been traditional for those in the East to work on beautifying their inner spiritual temples. It has been traditional for you to "strengthen the within." In the Western world, there has been a greater emphasis on the beautifying and harmonizing of the outer. Materialism on Earth has reached its zenith. There is not an equal distribution of the plenty that exists on your planet. As a result, people are starving while others are dumping milk and wheat into their lakes and oceans in the name of greater profit and imbalanced worship of materialism. *As I have said before, everything affects everything and everyone.* All of life is an interconnected web of living light and sacred sound energy. Just creating beauty on the inside and living nonesthetically causes imbalance and disharmonious states in the long term. Living in magnificently opulent homes and lifestyles, while totally ignoring the inner spiritual temple of your higher self (your heart and soul), leads many of you who have attained great wealth and fame to a tendency to destroy yourselves and your families though addiction, depression, and early death. Basically, in the eyes of the Divine Mother, you are a true spiritual genius when you find balance and achieve harmony in all areas of your being. It's not about just being a genius with art or music, but about embracing the spiritual harmony in your relationships and via your kind service to all who cross your path.

As I have mentioned before, it is a jolly good idea to focus the intent on inner and outer Feng Shui. All these help: to declutter, to create regular sacred space (through space clearing and sacred ceremony), to make time for wise story telling and celebration, and to spend time regularly with sacred fire. Helpful too, are conscious bathing, deep conscious breathing, and chanting the sacred sound OM or any other Divine Mantra of your choice such as "Sa Sekhem Sahu" or "Eternal Heart of Hathor." These practices will immediately help you into a state of grace, harmony, and beauty. They engender a beauty so deep and all, encompassing that it is truly heartfelt and therefore all-inclusive, not excluding the inner or the outer in its Divine embrace.

Bhole Baba, Babaji, says, "I am harmony, I am harmony, I am harmony." As you know, "as above, so below," the Divine Mother and Father energies are within the deepest core of each and everyone of you, so when they say they are harmony you can assume that is your deepest natural core resonance. May I inspire you to clear the cobwebs of disharmonious being, doing, and thinking and replacing the floppy disc of hell and conflict with the new harmonic (which is actually eternal heavenly harmony and balanced inner and outer beauty!)?

On the subject of the "D word", yes, that's right, the dreaded concept of detachment: let it be known that there is no spiritual or evolutionary progress of consciousness without it. Being the detached witness, the sakshi of All That Is, is one of the greatest keys of the Mystery School of Hathor and of any divine esoteric path to enlightenment and unity consciousness. Please note that as you practice detachment of your thoughts, emotions, and dramas, balance is crucially required so you don't use detachment to disengage from the essential fragrance of your inner compassion and responsibility; i.e., your ability to respond to the suffering and the pain of your inner climates and that of your brothers and sisters. Detachment does not mean being totally unfeeling and callous. *Herein comes my favorite distinction between absolute and relative reality. As a spiritual conscious warrior you keep one foot metaphorically in absolute reality within yourself while the other part, the personality self, is happily or unhappily engaging in relative reality. The absolute part of you is absolutely being the detached witness.* Meanwhile as you go about your daily activities, the relative part of you, your personality self, is engaging in relative reality that is dual in nature. In this part of your being, detachment may or may not be relevant based on moment-to-moment intuitive inner feeling and awareness.

> As you practice detachment . . . balance is crucially required so you don't use detachment to disengage from the essential fragrance of your inner compassion and responsibility.

It is the predisposition of your mind and your gut to latch on to addictive or obsessive thinking, feeling, or habitual behavior. As humans you are great creatures of habit. Often animals illustrate a greater intelligence to change habitual behavior if their survival depends on it. *Human beings on the other hand have a tendency to choose death in many cases as a preferred choice to changing habits and behavioral patterns to which they are deeply attached.* Choosing the familiar, however dysfunctional and idiotic it may be, from that which you truly desire and wish to create seems to come far more easily to many of you. The tricky thing here is that unless you go into deep states of inner healing, your subconscious and unconscious patterns continue to play havoc with your reality. This continues until you create time and space to bring these patterns to the surface, look at them, and then hopefully let them go if they are not serving your current agenda.

> Human beings ... have a tendency to choose death in many cases as a preferred choice to changing habits and behavioral patterns to which they are deeply attached.

Let us move on to one of the greatest pearls of wisdom that was practiced and inculcated in my Mystery School teachings in many dimensions. *Praise and gratitude bring miracles into your life.* In modern time it is not very fashionable for many of you, particularly in the Western world, to spend time in your inner and outer temples in prayer and ceremony. When you practice and celebrate the equinoxes, the solstices, and the thirteen Full Moons of your artificially created Gregorian calendar, you reconnect to the natural rhythm within you and your reality in a more balanced way. You can receive a lot of grace and flow through reconnecting and practicing sacred ritual and ceremony. The waxing and the waning of the moon as you know connects strongly to the magnetic aspect of your own electro-magnetic field of energy. The Moon has a powerful effect not just on the ebbing and flowing of your tides, but also on your emotional body, (represented by the water that comprises 90 percent of your physical temple).

Sunrise and sunset are powerful times to connect in praise and gratitude to the Father energies, the solar energy of your magnificent sun. Veneration to the moon is essentially connecting reverentially to the feminine energy of the Goddess and can deeply help to clear and heal your emotional body. If you keep awake all night on a full moon night and meditate and bathe in moonlight and possibly fast, you go through exponential healing and nurturing of your magnetic feminine aspect, whether you are a man or a woman, and powerful emotional body clearing.

This initiation of not sleeping all night sometimes helps (like fasting) to catapult you through to break habitual patterns into altered, and with intention, exalted states of consciousness. The ancient Vedantic students practiced, and still do, the deep reverence to the sun, which represents the element of fire and corresponds to the electrical aspect or the male aspect of your Being, your electro-magnetic field of energy. *So praise and gratitude are essential ingredients for the safe and joyous opening and healing of your human heart.* Your heart begins, through all these spiritual practices and through awareness and nurturing, to open slowly but surely to larger and larger expansive states of Being and Consciousness.

The heart can catapult you into magnificent new realities, probabilities, and possibilities. Its nature is intrinsically infinite, eternal, all forgiving, all encompassing, and pure unconditional love. So all the things that I observe mankind and womankind are hankering for, come to you so much more easily if you are willing to begin to nurture and open and listen to the lotus of your heart.

Have an attitude of gratitude that all that the river of your life brings to you moment-to-moment is to be revered and honored. This may shock you. But even the dark that crosses your path within or without can be bowed to, honored, and acknowledged. And then, of course, I recommend strongly for you to choose to ask it to leave politely, then, ask more strongly if it doesn't. Remember to do this three times and then, as per universal law of free will, any dark energy will be obliged to leave. If it does not, I suggest you run. As soon as you acknowledge, honor, and thank all that is occurring (be it people, places, things, or emotions), the more quickly you access your centeredness. It is easy to choose to engage or to disengage from a place of conscious, empowered, centered choice. It is the choice of your own inner authority as opposed to outer influences. Praise and gratitude need to occur moment-to-moment, and especially to the five elements that have created the bodies of your temple and your Earthly reality.

Just to reexplain how the mechanism of praise and gratitude gives you more of what you want: When you thank the universe for what you already have and are, you create a sacred space within and without yourself to receive a greater flow of that which you are focusing on, which in this case is thankfulness.

Sense of Humor

Your *sense of humor* can dissolve the greatest tumor (of sadness, pain, frustration). If you want to connect quickly to the energy of laughter and the cosmic joke Goddess of joy and exuberance of Ancient Egypt—no matter how dreadful or dramatic the dramas on the screen of your life may be—you can always choose to take a deep breathe and somehow find the funny side to the story line. Your sense of play and humor are one of the most valuable gifts on the path to higher consciousness and the alchemical transmutation and integration from the undesired pole of a polarity to the positive or desired aspect of the polarity. Laughter, for example, can take you smoothly out of sadness into lightness; out of anger into peace and possibly forgiveness. It is quite useful to write down a list of all that you fear in a given period of time or dislike, dread, hate, etc., and then practice laughter meditation regularly by choosing to laugh at the worst of your negative imaginings.

All enlightened gurus teach through laughter and of the importance of laughter to facilitate your accelerated lightening up. Your children are your great teachers on this subject and can take you into playing field states of joy and mirth at the drop of a hat. P. S.: don't forget to take your cat. Your animals have been gifted to you and can facilitate your lightening up as well. Once you tap into deep belly laughing, endorphins are naturally released in the system bringing about powerful healing and a change of frequency. Lord Krishna, Pan, and the Mayan Chuen energy are all wondrous examples from other streams of esoteric understanding that exemplify the power of humor.

Ultimately your reality is divine, cosmic play in the sacred Sanskrit texts known as Leela. Remember to connect your sense of humor to be heartfelt so that it will not be used as a weapon to hurt yourself or others in the name of innocent joking. As with all the qualities, it is important to use wisdom and awareness in the use and practice of the energy of humor. Remembering cultural differences and respecting the boundaries of others become relevant in the effective reaping of this magnificent quality.

Innocence

When you become merrier and are capable of seeing the most serious scenario in your life from its funny side, then you come easily into the energy of innocence and harmlessness. I observe with a lot of dismay that a vast part of humanity is suffering currently from deep guilt and shame, which are intrinsic parts of the paradigm of the Age of Pisces. While you carry the burden of blame and shame on your backs you are debilitated in many ways. One of the definitions to understand guilt is that it is a lesson not learned. Guilt and shame are not the same as atonement, forgiveness, and discernment. Every time you find yourself feeling ashamed or shaming another, check yourself, take a deep breath, and carefully steer the light of your heartfelt awareness to the ultimate innocence of your soul energy and the pristine purity of that energy reflected in others, irrespective of what is happening at their periphery or yours. Remember that just because you see others and yourself as ultimately pure emanations of the same Divine Unified Field of Consciousness, does not mean that you do not discriminate and even at times oppose what is happening on the periphery, e.g., war, deceit, or manipulation and control. So the heart may choose to have a deep understanding of the intrinsic innocence in all things, while the personality self may act consciously through heartfelt guidance to, at the same time, take action to oppose where soul wisdom dictates.

When you are in a state of innocence you are able to approach things with the mind and heart of a child. This means that you let go of any preconceptions. In the eyes of the Divine Mother you are always blameless, faultless, pure, and true emanations of Source. No matter what your naughty little personality and mind are up to, the Divine Mother forgives and atones. She is there to lift you, help you, inspire you, and when necessary carry you through the ebb and flow of lifetimes. However, she too has a personality self and her heart and love for you may dictate stern lessons being meted out for behavioral patterns that do not conform to her universal laws. As Goddess Hathor, I am a particularly benevolent and compassionate aspect of the Divine Mother who speaks to you and teaches you through the frequencies of celebration, love, and joy.

My sister aspect of Sekhmet is a good example, together with Kali, of a more disciplinarian, warlike aspect of the Goddess/Divine Mother energies of the universe. Aspects of the Divine such as Sekhmet and Lord Shiva represent a high order of destruction of that which is not in alignment with Divine Will and Universal Sacred Law. Their energies only destroy or remove within free will that which is an impediment to the initiate's soul journey to Higher Consciousness.

In the eyes of the Divine, all things are equal and loved in equal measure whether you be an ant, a criminal, an angel, or the Holy of Holies. But as I have repeatedly reminded you this does not mean that you get off the hook vis-a-vis the law of cause and effect. The more you start getting an awareness of the relative and the absolute and the differences of the agenda of your mind versus the wisdom of your soul/heart energy, the more simple it becomes to take responsibility for the creation of your reality and to start creating preferred scenarios. *So innocence is a key to powerful conscious co-creation and effortless manifestation.* While you carry heavy loads of "should nots, cannots, not allowed" and so on, the possibility of innocent, childlike, effortless, spontaneous co-creation from the heart moment-to-moment becomes an impossibility.

Serving All of Life

On the pathway to heartfelt spiritual success, your service to self and others and all of life is imperative. When you see through spiritual practice and the eyes of the Higher Mind or Buddhi, your spiritual intelligence automatically begins to flower into service-oriented altruistic consciousness. When you meditate, if you do so correctly, your heart begins to heal, open, and overflow with love, and this unconditional love and compassion naturally spill out and encompass everyone and everything that comes in your path. You become one with the unified field of consciousness. You become the unique Christ in your own right when you begin to see all beings and all of life as divine aspects of the Divine Self, the Unified Field of Consciousness that is within you and is reflected outside of you in all things.

The great divinely guided entity Doctor Usui discovered (when he rediscovered the power of universal life-force energy which he called Reiki) the power of service to "all that is." One of his main Reiki ideals is, *"Just for today I will do my work honestly."* This work he understood in his enlightened state is not just the outer work and service in the world but also very much the inner work—the work of waking up connecting to an evolutionary progression of consciousness and a restrengthening of reconnection with the Divine.

Here I would like to clarify that just as all of you are actually one unified field of energy that has split up to become universes, planets, individuals, plants, animals, and so on similarly, based on the "as above, so below" Universal Law, the Divine too is perceived by you as the Divine Mother, the Divine Father, various aspects of the Sacred Male and Female archetypal energies, Gods, Goddesses, and avatars, which are direct emanations of Source in human form (e.g., Babaji, Mother Mary, archangels, and so on).

Mahakaruna, or great compassion, as powerful Tibetan initiates of the spiritual school of Av understood "alokiteschwara," is not just feeling empathetic or compassionate towards your fellow human beings and the animal and plant kingdom. Mahakaruna implies taking action to swerve over and love humanity and life, using the balance of Buddha (i.e., higher intellect and heartfelt wisdom). As you now know and actually have always known, sometimes the heart chooses to say "no" or walk away. Using intuition, your feeling body and your gut instinct to help you decide when to serve, how much to serve, and when to not participate is crucial in balanced, spiritually oriented service to life.

The Maha Avatar Babaji in his incarnation on Earth in the 70s on your planet kept stressing the importance of karma yoga or the yoga of work worship in this coming time of colossal change and transmutation. He talked about the great purification that has to occur for Earth and her peoples to rebalance the pollution and devastation of the Age of Darkness. Thirteen thousand years of manipulation, control, survival-of-the-fittest, and war! The Divine ultimately always proves victorious over the darkness. Even if you take a tiny candle into a huge hall of darkness, you dispel the darkness. So incarnations such as Babaji and Jesus have come to teach us and help us reinstate the light in your reality now.

Service and sharing and the honoring of all people as ultimately equal is exponential in transmutation of the darkness within and without to the Light. *The more you serve all of life with a happy, joyful heart, letting go of resentment and stress, the faster you begin to receive the unlimited gifts of the universe.* Synergy, synchronicity, and miracles become second nature. Every encounter of every moment is a grand opportunity to raise the vibrational frequency to a harmonic of joy, peace, generosity and love.

As the Goddess of love, celebration, and plenty, I want to make it very clear (in case some of you have forgotten) that all work is Sacred. Whether you be a sweeper or a King, you can make your work holy, whole, and complete. You can raise work to a higher level of exalted Divinity through intention, humility, detachment and through lovingly offering it up to the Highest Within you and within all of life everywhere. The wings of Isis embrace you in love and Divine cooperation; and your asking and remembering amplify her energies of benediction and grace in your life. *Please do remember to keep one foot in detached witnessing no matter how important you think your job is.* The universal law of paradox insists that though your work is magnificent and in service to the Divine, on another level you are doing nothing and humility is important.

To go around as a spiritual New Age type with a lot of stress about saving the world and being overburdened in your tasks by God and the universe is faulty understanding of the nature of divine play. Balance your being and your doing. Balance your beingness between your role in the world and your centeredness in the un-manifest temple of silence and none-doing. This will catapult you and many others into ecstatic states of bliss and spiritual achievement.

Balance your being and your doing. Balance your beingness between your role in the world and your centeredness in the un-manifest temple of silence and none-doing.

Please remember to stay grounded in your manifestations on Earth. The pyramidal energy through invocation greatly helps to ground manifestation in your physical realm, no matter how high the consciousness that is to be grounded. The pyramid very much honors the power of four and the power of honoring the four directions, which are essential building blocks in your known physical reality.

12

ENERGY

UNDERSTANDING OF THE SCIENCE of energy is no longer optional on the path of heartfelt spiritualization of your reality. Life-force energy (chi or prana) is electromagnetic frequency which is capable of being changed and manipulated. This energy does not die, it changes form. It is ever-moving and eternal. The movement is in spirals and waves and not straight lines. Van Gogh was a high initiate who understood this and painted the stars in spirals in his famous paintings. The energy can be compressed, diverted, changed in temperature, etc., and although invisible to the normal human eye in this relative reality, on this third-dimensional planet the results of the changes are detectable.

In relation to the human heart it can be expanded and filled and nurtured as you choose to bring in more and more of this life-force energy. As your DNA evolves from two to twelve strands many of your multidimensional coding patterns are being fired up—reignited after what is in human terms a rather long period of time. You can choose to bring in more of the sacred high-energy frequencies (such as Reiki, for example) and they will then help you to heal your heart and regenerate your tissues and cells.

The understanding and conscious use of energy is of great importance in this accelerated time. Why? Because as you go through intensity and more intensity of the initiations which are the current dramas in your life coming up one after the other with no breaks, it may oftentimes feel like you are going mad. All of time is merging into this grand time, going beyond linear time and space into Unity Consciousness. But before you have both feet firmly established in the fifth-dimensional frequency waves of unlimited being and becoming, creator gods and goddesses that you are, you must clear your DNA, your memory banks, and your karma until such time as you reunite fully to the blossoming of the pure potential energy of your soul.

All residual unresolved unembraced and unhealed karmic patterns are coming up in relentless succession for all of you who are still mainly operating within a relative reality orientation. For those of you who are grounding states of pure enlightened being and becoming, the laws of karma and linear time and space are transcended. However for many of you, your reality is mainly operating within linear time and space and a part of your being is moving into fifth-dimensional reality.

The Goddess energy is here on Earth in a powerful, dynamic way (after eons of having taken a little bit of a back seat), to empower you to clear your fields of energy so that you may harmoniously and easily move into the new frequencies of Christ consciousness that are strongly impulsing Earth and her peoples now.

Energy, as I keep repeating, can neither be created nor destroyed. It is what the ancient Vedas call Chiti Shakti. The building blocks of manifest reality. As you begin to cultivate the deeper and more intimate relationship and awareness of your energy fields and their interaction with the energy fields of others, you become more and more enlightened, empowered, and free of the tyranny of the past and the future.

As your beloved author Eckhard Tolle says, the great power of the Now is achieved. Let me give you an example how energy awareness can shift you instantaneously from being a victim to being a heartfelt conscious co-creator. If you are unaware that your energy fields are, for example, swimming in the energy of anger or fear, then you will keep repeating dramas that you look at and say, "I didn't want it to be like this!" Your unconscious or subconscious mind will continue to create or destroy. The understanding of the energies of your mind, your heart, your electromagnetic field, and of your universal life-force energy is of utmost importance in the journey back to the within: to the main line of the energy source-field which is within you, within you, within you.

This all sounds very complicated. The paradox is that the more complicated something is the more quickly you can go to its antidote by shifting your attention to the polarity, which in this case is the polarity of complexity—that is right—intend simplicity. *Similarly by asking your inner self where your energy is, if you get the answer it is in the energy of anger, you can then (through the law of attention plus intention equals manifestation) choose the energy of peace, or energy of love, or of forgiveness.*

Please do remember that when it comes to forgiveness, it is sometimes quite crucial that you release in safety any anger around the issue before you can achieve true lasting forgiveness. I have given you ways earlier in safe releasing of anger, which are for example: dancing it out, writing it out, singing it out, brisk walking in nature, and hitting a pillow without causing harm to yourself. There are many healing modalities that you could also choose to help your anger management.

> Please do remember that when it comes to forgiveness, it is sometimes quite crucial that you release in safety any anger around the issue before you can achieve true lasting forgiveness.

I, Goddess Hathor, find the term anger management most amusing. Stanislavski's holotropic breathing, vivation breathing, Leonard Orr's rebirthing modality, and psychic surgery are some of the myriad healing pathways you can choose to release in safety negative emotions such as anger and fear. Please note that ultimately emotions are neither negative nor positive, but within the relative realm the so-called "negative emotions" trigger cause and effect the same way as do the positive emotions.

The integration of the male and female polarities within you and outside of you lead to you becoming more and more whole and complete. The understanding and awareness, and the balance of the energies of male and female, are useful in the inner alchemy of your ultimately androgyny. My symbol of Hathor (which marries the Sun and Moon energies), is a powerful symbolism of the divine play of the male and female archetypal energies of the universe within you and reflected in your cosmos.

The understanding of energy in this heartfelt esoteric way is, please note, not to be a great intellectual analysis, or hypothesis. It is rather a very gentle awareness acknowledgement. The subtler this awareness of the divine play of different energies within and without, the greater is the catapulting of your consciousness on the evolutionary ladder. Your indigenous shamans of past times understood energy very well. As I have already mentioned to you, for example, if you wish to sit and purify by the sacred element of fire and it is not possible within your circumstance to do so literally in a given moment, you always have the powerful option of invoking and expanding the energy of fire within you.

The energy of love is the most exalted energy in the universe of the manifest. Your human hearts have been created out of deep love of the Divine Mother and the Divine Father in total likeness to their own magnificent cosmic hearts. Your human hearts are waking up into reconnection and expansion with their intergalactic brothers and sisters. Heart energy is the easy way to come into the dance of synergy, synchronicity, flow, joy, and celebration. True celebration requires genuine heartfeltness.

> **The energy of love is the most exalted energy in the universe of the manifest.**

I would like to point out the difference between unconditional heart energy and love that is always all-encompassing rather than exclusive and considers the higher good of the individual, group, or issue. This does not mean that as a unique individual you do not honor your individuality and that you may not love a specific other in a special way. Your mind thinks that both the above-mentioned perspectives cannot be practiced at the same time but for the heart, this is easy.

Romantic love is a wondrous energy that many of you are most enamored by, tantalized with, and have endless chats with Cupid about. Cupid is a busy little cherub on Earth. Romantic love is the brilliant story of humanity of heights of passion, golden creativity, and great woes. *I currently observe that the vast majority of you are broken-hearted.* Your education, cultural encoding, conditioning, and media oftentimes propagate unrealistic and imbalanced romantic scenarios. All these sort of adventures are valid on the grand journey back to the temple of unconditional compassionate all-encompassing Christ Love. This all-encompassing love is ultimately the true nature of your human heart temple within you.

As you become more open-hearted and balanced in heaven and Earth energies, with your heart as the meeting point of this Divine Alchemy, your love becomes more and more all-encompassing, unconditional, natural, and flowing. *In this state of greater and greater centeredness and Christ consciousness, i.e., unity consciousness, you become capable of loving more than one entity deeply at the same time.* This state when balanced, when truthful, when present to the Now moment and open is totally innocent and simple. This is not an excuse to hurt the ones we love through cheating, lying, and deceitfulness. All parties concerned require a high degree of spiritual maturity and need to be in agreement with whatever the rule of this particular love game may be and may be allowed total freedom to take responsibility for any pain they may feel and choose to walk away from the situation. As you know, the Gods and Goddesses, for example of India, had many wives and husbands, many consorts, but their consciousness was in a state of deep awareness and unity consciousness.

Nefertiti and Akhenaton were created by their parents, Ay and Tiya, who were immortals on Earth. They were hundreds of years old and came from a very high level of consciousness, stepping down the fifth-dimensional energies of Sirius. Nefertiti and Akhenaton were created to step down the Christ-conscious energies within physicality on Earth at the time. They were brother and sister. This is probably a very difficult concept for many of you as you read this to digest with your minds. It is not an understanding you can come to through intellectualization. In ordinary relative reality, the cohabiting of siblings is naturally not desirable or healthy or allowed in most societies. The important point here is the state of consciousness of the entities involved.

The Qualities of
Openhearted Beingness are:

1. Nonjudgment

2. Simplicity

3. Courage

4. Vulnerability

5. Allowance and acceptance

6. Giving and sharing

7. Silence and peace

8. Beauty and harmony

9. Detachment

10. Praise and gratitude

11. Sense of humor

12. Innocence

13. Serving all of life (service)

14. Whatever makes your heart sing

15. Inspiration and creativity

16. Being here now

17. Unity Consciousness

18. Embracement

19. Highest Good of all concerned

20. Unconditional Love

21. Inspiration and creativity

22. Responsibility

CONCLUSION BY
THE GODDESS HATHOR

THANK YOU FOR SHARING this time with me. You have made me, Goddess Hathor, feel your energy and my grace and benediction will pour into your beautiful jewel-like hearts within your free will and your own unique rhythm and timing. *You cannot imagine how much the Divine Mother loves you and how much she wishes to shower you with celestial wisdom and unlimited empowerment and easement.*

Please allow me to allow you to dance into the freedom, the expansion and the celebration of your heart temple. If you do not give me permission, all my power and all my love cannot come to you no matter how much I, as your beloved Divine Mother, yearn to lift you from the mire. My heartfelt prayer is that all of humanity will allow the Divine Mother to heal the wounds and step up grace for your accelerated healing and awakening into Christ-conscious frequencies of love and light. I have given you many keys to the healing and reactivation of your Christ heart. Your heart is the doorway to higher consciousness. It is the meeting point for the marrying of heaven and earth within you.

The times to come will step up in intensity and confusion, which is core-fusion, and will make way for new patterns to emerge. The collapse of the old systems is imperative to make way for a higher order. The questions to ask are, "Who am I?" and, "What do I choose to co-create in this glorious time of the ending of time?" The exalted question to ask is, "How can I create heaven on Earth for myself and all others?" And the most powerful question of all is, "What is the highest good of all concerned in each moment of Now, in each decision that I make, and in each encounter I experience with all of life everywhere?" The word evil is the word live reversed. I inspire you and impulse you, while I honor your freedom of choice, to choose life, to choose creation, to choose wisely, to allow six billion humans their ancient eyes to the eternal and yet paradoxically pristine new reality of Christ-consciousness for Gaia and all of life here now.

The word evil is the word live reversed.

The Divine Mother has reminded you through this sacred missive of all that you already know within the silent wisdom of your inner temple. All knowledge and wisdom of past, present, and future is within you and can be reactivated.

By connecting and revering the sacred elements and working consciously with the archetypal energies of the universe and through the simple and pleasurable practices of prayer, mantram repetition, chanting, and sacred ceremony, you may all open to your glorious potential of the inner divine pharaoh energy of being and becoming. I bestow a shower of Rashmi, celestial moonlight or sunlight upon you. (Rashmi in Sanskrit means moonlight and sunlight.) This book has been encoded to fire your encodings and activate your DNA exponentially within your free will and your own individual unique choice of timing. The cosmic intergalactic union of your brothers and sisters from other realities and dimensions and the reunion with the departed loved ones awaits you. It is time to give up the shackles of limitation, control, manipulation, and fear.

RASHMI'S CONCLUSION

It is no coincidence that you have picked up this book, as you have been attracted to it through the laws of intention, attraction, and morphogenic resonance. The Goddess would like me to share with you that this work encapsulates her living light energy fields and so just being with the book can heal you, shift you, and facilitate powerful emotional body clearing. All this can occur without you even reading a line. However, based on the strong way in which I have been shifted and cleared of a lot of my emotional, obsolete garbage, I would highly recommend that you do work with this material as you are guided. I would also recommend you following your own unique rhythm and timing when working with this material so as to not overdo the emotional processing.

In this intense time, where the old meets the new, the Age of Darkness gives way to the Age of Light. Our consciousness individually is being raised at a very rapid rate to match the frequencies of being a fully enlightened being. It is imperative that we fasten our spiritual seat belts and get ready to change and change and change on the Express Route to waking up.

As of today, the last day of 2009, we as humans are experiencing national and global economic meltdown and a collapsing of many of our systems—political, ecological, social, and cultural. The time for uniting these different streams of our beingness with our spiritual self, and letting go of treating them as separate from our innate esoteric inner knowingness, has come.

In my recent time in the United States, in the run-up to Obama being installed as president of the United States, I realised that this is one of the many brilliant signs that light workers all over the world need not despair in this darkest moment of human destiny—before the Dawning of an Age of Light.

One of the most powerful ways to ride the current dramatic waves of change I have found in my life to be:

> **To follow impeccably my intuition through my intention—to align with the highest divinity within me at all times as far as possible.**

I no longer question how illogical some of my movements and decisions seem to my startled human mind. If my guidance is to jump on an airplane, call someone, be somewhere, or say something—no matter how idiotic it might seem to myself or others—I work with unconditional heart-love energy to augment my inner voice.

BE STILL AND KNOW

Nothing in this book is new but that is how things are anyways! You know all of this wisdom and so much more, but oftentimes we forget! The energy of love and unconditional acceptance of the Divine Mother is strongly encapsulated in this book. I trust that you will continue to work with this material and that we will meet again and again as immortals on many expansive stages, of "Time/ Space Continuums," to create and celebrate the amazing wonders of being and becoming!

Rashmi Khilnani
December 31, 2009
Charlottesville, Virginia

In Praise of the Divine Mother

O Celestial Mother of the Universe!

Thy Hair the Milky Way and a thousand Shining Stars!
Thy Body this Beautiful Earth Jewel Gaia!
Thy Breath the Cosmic Winds of the Solar System!
Thy Grace an ocean of compassion and acceptance!
Thy Caress the Wondrous Soothing Balm
To ease my heart's distress!

Let me follow thy Heart's Tune, O Wondrous Mistress!
May the Goddess Energy be invoked strongly
In the hearts of men and women Now!
May the Feminine Principle of Holding, Being, Allowing, and
Embracing All That Is Manifest,
Unfurl Here Now!

Thy Multifaceted Forms inspire me!
Our tumultuous Soul Journeys are impulsed to follow Thee.
May thy Effulgence and Omniscient Love
Become One with Me.
May I keep singing and dancing Thy Praises
As a Heart-song of Joy and Glee.

If the Earth changes are to happen,
Let me be On Mother Gaia
One of thy wondrous trees.
Thy Grace and Benediction
Bring me to where I Am At One and Free.
Praise, Love, Infinite Gratitude, and Salutations to thee!

O Celestial Mother of the Universe to Thee, to Thee, to Thee!

—Rashmi

ACKNOWLEDGMENTS

My HEARTFELT THANKS to my Earth book team. . . .

To Amravati for her unending encouragement and her transcriptions.

To Cynthia Moore for her loving support and wonderful editing.

To Robert Friedman for his patience and friendship and for agreeing to do the final edits.

To Enoch for his wisdom in buying the computer years before the book was channeled and his strong belief that it would be.

To my Babaji soulmate Leonard Orr for his participation in this project and his ongoing loving inspiration.

To Jonathan Friedman for the beautiful graphics.

I would also like to thank my celestial team, especially Babaji, my ever-loving friend and guide, and the Divine Mother in her heart Goddess mode: Hathor.

Thank you, guys. Without you this work would not be manifesting in this wondrous moment of Now!

BIOGRAPHY OF
RASHMI KHILNANI

RASHMI KHILNANI was born in the designer city Chandigarh, India, and was conceived and spent the first six years of her life in Cairo, Egypt.

Having lived and established a global business network with her former husband, in the last fifteen years she has gone on to studying and teaching with world-renowned avatars, gurus, and teachers and has become a specialist in energy medicine. She is on the forefront of bringing the ancient Mystery School teachings of Egypt, India, Tibet, China, and the teachings of the Essenes into current time and making these teachings simple and accessible to people at all levels of soul journeying.

Rashmi teaches and practices several healing modalities and has taught Reiki Masters, doctors, scientists, and people from many walks of life the secrets of the Mystery School teachings. She is a global metaphysical teacher, urban shaman, international lecturer, artist, seminar leader, and TV personality.

She utilizes her Goddess-given gifts of psychic intuitive channeling, sound, light, breath, and vibration to help shift and heal individuals and groups and conducts ceremonies for morphogenic global heart healing. She works closely with the Divine Father aspect—Maha Avatar Babaji—and the Goddess Hathor for heart healing. Having met influential personalities all her life in the realm of politics, spirituality, and the arts, she seeks to serve the Ascended Masters in bringing a spiritualization and heartfeltness of unconditional love and unity consciousness to people of all walks of life. She also works and trains her Reiki Master students in the healing and rebalancing of the sacred elements and Mother Earth herself.

Rashmi's connection to the Goddess Hathor goes back to when she was two years of age playing around the sands of the Great Pyramid of Giza and the sacred Sphinx. She has particular intuitive knowledge of the secrets of the pyramids and the Star People such as the Hathor Beings in the higher realms of Venus. In spite of her cosmic orientation, she is down to earth, grounded, and teaches through practicality, truth, love, and simplicity, and a great sense of humor.

The Goddess Hathor in the last few years has requested that Rashmi (who is one of the only Initiating Master Channels into the Mystery School of Hathor in current time on Earth) re-creates a school for her teachings not only for Reiki Masters and practitioners but for all spiritual aspirants everywhere.

At this time, leading up to 2012, the ending of the Mayan calendar, the photonic energy is making it possible and probable for many souls across the globe to open up to the pure heartfelt frequencies of unity consciousness and unconditional love, which are the hallmark of the Mystery School of Hathor.

Rashmi has had graphic recall during initiations into Sekhem, Seichim, Seichem, and Karuna® Reiki Mastery, of lifetimes as

Egyptian high priestess and other powerful Egyptian esoteric life-times. She has appeared in the media relating to her pioneering psychic feng shui work and her work as an interior designer. Currently her "Heart of Hathor" seminars across the globe are taking precedence.

As she has done in previous lifetimes in Golden Ages in Egypt, she is being impulsed in this moment of Now to create a pioneering concept and centers of international spiritual community where art, love, and heaven on Earth can flourish.

Through the channeling of this sacred work, the many pearls of wisdom and gifts of the Goddess have been showered on Rashmi and her Earthly book team. She feels tremendous love, gratitude, and humility for being part of such a deep and expansive ocean of grace and love. Rashmi would like from the bottom of her heart to share this celestial transmission with you, her fellow brothers and sisters.

To find out more about Rashmi log on to
www.reiki-energy-mastery.com